ALSO BY FREDRIK DeBOER

The Cult of Smart

HOW ELITES ATE THE SOCIAL JUSTICE MOVEMENT

FREDRIK DeBOER

SIMON & SCHUSTER

New York   Toronto   London   Sydney   New Delhi

Simon & Schuster
1230 Avenue of the Americas
New York, NY 10020

First Simon & Schuster hardcover edition September 2023

SIMON & SCHUSTER and colophon are registered trademarks of Simon & Schuster, Inc.

For information about special discounts for bulk purchases, please contact
Simon & Schuster Special Sales at 1-866-506-1949 or business@simonandschuster.com.

The Simon & Schuster Speakers Bureau can bring authors to your live event.
For more information or to book an event, contact the
Simon & Schuster Speakers Bureau at 1-866-248-3049 or
visit our website at www.simonspeakers.com.

Interior design by Ruth Lee-Mui

Manufactured in the United States of America

1   3   5   7   9   10   8   6   4   2

Library of Congress Cataloging-in-Publication Data

Names: deBoer, Fredrik, author.
Title: How elites ate the social justice movement / by Fredrik deBoer.
Description: First Simon & Schuster hardcover edition. | New York :
Simon & Schuster, [2023] | Includes bibliographical references.
Identifiers: LCCN 2023013996 (print) | LCCN 2023013997 (ebook) | ISBN 9781668016015
(hardcover) | ISBN 9781668016022 (paperback) | ISBN 9781668016039 (ebook)
Subjects: LCSH: Social movements—United States. | Social justice—United States. |
Elite (Social sciences)—United States. | United States—Social conditions—21st century.
Classification: LCC HN65 .D345 2023 (print) | LCC HN65 (ebook) |
DDC 303.3/720973—dc23/eng/20230621
LC record available at https://lccn.loc.gov/2023013996
LC ebook record available at https://lccn.loc.gov/2023013997

ISBN 978-1-6680-1601-5
ISBN 978-1-6680-1603-9 (ebook)

For Nick Tucci
domani, brother

CONTENTS

HOW ELITES ATE
THE SOCIAL JUSTICE
MOVEMENT

INTRODUCTION

Spend enough time in activist spaces and you start to see the patterns unfold before you, like a skipping record. I am now some twenty-five years into a career as a part-time organizer. Some years I've organized more, some I've organized less, and I took a break during grad school, but I've tried to get involved one way or another since I first became politically conscious as a teenager. Over that time, I have watched the same dynamics play out again and again, dedicated organizers falling into the same sad patterns that obstruct progress. The victories have been real, but the failures have been more frequent and bitter, sometimes resulting in the fracturing of groups and friendships. There are many stories I could tell, and in this book I will tell some of them.

But when I think of the pathologies of political organizing, I often think first of an example that's quite trivial, where the stakes were very low, and yet, to me, it says something about how the left works. And the story is a little funny, which is appropriate, as there is a tragicomic element to our history, to the left's recent history as a would-be mass movement.

When I was a master's student at the University of Rhode Island

(URI), some undergraduate students committed themselves to a political action that surprised and inspired me. At the time, in 2010, there was no real LGBTQ+ center for students on campus, despite such centers having become common on campuses across the country. To student activists at URI, this lack of a central safe place for LGBTQ+ students to congregate was reflective of a broader failure of the school's higher administration to show respect to their community. These feelings of a lack of safety were not hard to understand; to pick a salient example, same-sex marriage would not come to Rhode Island for a few more years.

The students decided to do something about it. In the fall, activists occupied a section of URI's library for eight days, refusing to surrender the space until their demands were heard. At the end of those eight days, and after several rounds of negotiation with the school's brass, the activists could declare victory. They had won their major demands, including the creation of a shiny new LGBTQ+ center.

You can certainly question the efficacy of what the students had won. Central to the administration's concessions was the creation of a diversity czar of the type that is now ubiquitous in higher education. I have, in the past, expressed great skepticism about the ability of these mushrooming administrative roles to prompt real positive change. But the basic demand of a space for LGBTQ+ students was a sound one, and I was charmed and excited by the willingness of the students to provoke significant confrontation to get what they wanted. It was exactly the kind of activism I had long admired and missed.

I had been a young activist once myself. In high school, I helped organize a little around gay rights issues, which were then (in the late 1990s) still rather fringe. I really dove in when I got to college. The 9/11 attacks rocked the country and put us into a tailspin of nationalism, militarism, and paranoia. I confess that even I was not totally immune to the desire for revenge; for about four hours after the attacks, I marinated in a pleasant fantasy of good versus evil. But I was raised in a leftist household and had heard the history of my country and the evil it had done, and I was not seduced. When I got to Central Connecticut State University (CCSU) in 2002, the Iraq invasion was still a year away, but everyone knew that war was coming. Some of us rose up to meet it. I organized first at campus, through CCSU's progressive student union, and then later hooked on with activists out of Hartford. Most of what happened from there fell under the auspices of the shaggy umbrella organization Connecticut United for Peace, affectionately known as "CutUP."

By 2004, I was punching the clock every week, organizing against the war. One particular march through Hartford seemed to take an almost impossible amount of time and effort to pull off. Much of activism is mundane, tedious, and thankless; there's little glamour in being the one to rent the porta-potties for a rally, but it is essential. The city government in Hartford was making all of that much harder. They had come up with a list of absurd demands for how our march should function, which was something of a reversal of the relationship between government and organizers. Most pressingly, they had said that we would have to pay Hartford cops, at overtime rates, to come and provide "security." (Security we of course did not want.) We had no intention of paying a bunch of cops to come oppress us—and anyway, we never could have afforded to.

Eventually we were able to get a lawyer from the American Civil Liberties Union (ACLU) to make a few inquiries into the constitutionality of what the city was asking, which seemed to rattle the cage of the mayor's office. They dropped their absurd requirements and gave us our permits, though in a petty little assertion of their power they had changed the term "antiwar march" from our application to "peace rally" on the permit. I was delighted to have my name appear on the permit, and we pulled off the march, with several hundred people coming to demand an end to a senseless war. When the march was over, I felt real pride. I was also totally exhausted.

I will detail some of the particular failings of the anti–Iraq war movement later in this book. For now, it's enough to say that the experience taught me that "the movement" could be right about everything and still be an absolute mess. I spent three years watching as opposition to a ruinous war of aggression devolved into factionalization, accusations of racism and bigotry, attempts by fringe groups to commandeer events, and bitter disputes about goals and tactics. We expended energy fighting an internecine war at home instead of opposing the brutal one on the other side of the world. The question of Israel and Palestine, seemingly a distinct issue from Iraq, bled into every meeting, every teach-in, every debate, and I don't need to tell you that these fights were ugly. To make matters worse, we had no effect at all on the US government's actions. I believed, and still believe, that protest is necessary and righteous even when it achieves nothing tangible; we could not let the US invasion of Iraq go by without making a mark in history through our resistance. But still, everywhere I looked I saw failure.

And so, soon after that last rally, I moved to Chicago and put antiwar activism behind me. I was spent emotionally, and anyway, it was time for my postcollegiate life to begin. I passed through the next several years in the typical hedonistic style of someone in his mid-twenties, drinking and drugging and hooking up and working a series of meaningless, low-paying jobs. When my late twenties rolled around, I found myself in the teeth of the recession that followed the 2008 financial meltdown with a sad résumé and a BA in English. Not knowing what else to do, I went to grad school, and that's how I found myself on campus during the URI student occupation of the library.

You can, I hope, imagine why I saw so much to admire in their actions. Organizing had been central to my emotional life, and I had left it behind feeling hopeless and despondent. I was eager to be inspired, and suddenly I was. I also hope you can imagine why I was disappointed when, after their victory, I asked one of the young activists about their next goal, and he answered, "We're fighting the Four Loko ban!"

From fighting for recognition of a large group of vulnerable people to demanding the right to continue buying an alcoholic beverage notorious for its extreme caffeine content . . . it seemed like a step backward, to put it mildly. Of course, they were kids, and there's no need to harp on the misguided choices of a bunch of young idealists who hadn't yet become politically experienced. That conversation just happened to exemplify my sense that American progressive movements are forever wandering from the righteous to the ridiculous.

In 2020, a year that was sold at the time as a moment of unique political foment—as a "reckoning"—we saw the American progressive movement drift from the essential to the inconsequential, from the material to the illusory, in much the same way.

Early that year, an unprecedented global pandemic bloomed in front of our eyes. The novel coronavirus Covid-19 exploded out from China and across the face of the globe in the span of a few months. There have been deadlier diseases, and there have been diseases that have wrought more havoc, but there had never before been a disease that so took advantage of a globalized and interconnected Earth, of our now-small world. The virus rocked the world economy, sending us tumbling into a micro-depression, as hundreds of thousands of deaths and millions of infections taxed the world's working population and as restrictions and quarantines designed to stop the spread torpedoed economic activity. Many of us were forced to stay at home for weeks, where all we could do was read more bad news and worry.

Americans were on edge. A presidential election year could only fan those flames. Donald Trump, one of the most controversial presidents in American history, faced an emboldened progressive movement and dissent within the ranks of the party and political ideology he ostensibly led. His constant gaffes and imbroglios, including his widely criticized handling of the pandemic, helped chip away at whatever legitimacy he held as a popular-vote loser who had been elected under a cloud of controversy in 2016. Meanwhile, the Bernie Sanders campaign of 2016 had energized a new generation of socialist activists, such as those in the Democratic Socialists of America, and early in 2020 it appeared that Sanders's return primary candidacy was genuinely viable. The country was simmering.

On May 25, that simmer was brought to a boil. A forty-six-year-old Black man named George Floyd was confronted by Minneapolis police after a store clerk accused him of passing a counterfeit twenty-dollar bill. Derek Chauvin and three other officers removed Floyd from a car and threw him to ground. Chauvin then proceeded to lean on Floyd's neck with his knee for almost nine minutes, killing him. A cell phone video of the attack circulated immediately thanks to social media. The shocking footage incensed much of the country and galvanized the left. Calls for justice rang from seemingly every corner, as even traditionally apolitical corporations and risk-averse politicians took part. Protesters flooded the streets demanding not just the prosecution of Chauvin and his fellow officers but for a total remaking of society's relationship to race. Several of these protests exploded into riots. Black Lives Matter signs became ubiquitous in the real world, and support for the protests became inescapable online.

In response to this communal demand for change, America's institutions spun into action. Universities, foundations, and nonprofits drafted statements in support of racial justice and began implementing programs to diversify their workforces and student bodies. An army of young activists were hired into academia, public service, and the nonprofit sector.

Grandiose plans for total reconstruction of our society were devised. Reforms for education and government were proposed. And behind all of these ideas came an insistent, angry, insatiable demand: justice could wait no longer.

And then, very little happened.

No major federal legislation would result from the upheaval of 2020. Some cities and states enacted modest criminal-justice reforms, but many of these were later quietly rolled back. In Minneapolis, where Floyd's murder had taken place, the drift over time was telling: the city council first voted to abolish and replace its police department, then later changed the reforms to simple budget cuts, then later enacted an increase in funding to the very department it had recently set about to dissolve.

Where was the change that had been demanded? Yes, many from Black and other minority backgrounds found themselves with scholarships or jobs that did not exist prior to the civil unrest, but they were drawn largely from the upwardly mobile professional and managerial classes to begin with. Cultural institutions relentlessly looked to reward people from marginalized groups, but the impact of these efforts is hard to see; there is little connection between Netflix beating the bushes to find Black and Hispanic stand-up comics to give specials to and the quality of day-to-day life in minority neighborhoods. It's also fair to ask whether the army of new young bureaucrats hired into colleges and thinktanks could ever actually accomplish real change. Murals and signs are all well and good in and of themselves, but they serve little purpose if not part of a broader effort for actual material change. The calls from establishment politicians for justice were simply folded into business as usual.

Political change is hard; progressive political change is even harder. The inertia of established systems is remarkable, and we need never be overly critical of activists for failing to achieve change, given the inherent difficulties involved. That said, the lack of change that stemmed from the largest explosion of political consciousness in my lifetime is remarkable. The term "reckoning" was invoked again and again, and yet we don't seem to have reckoned with any of our problems in any meaningful way. What happened? This book is an attempt to answer that question. And to answer it, we will have to look back into the past, to see how this failure was merely the latest in a long string of failures for progressive social movements. I will diagnose why the default state of such movements is failure and suggest steps toward a future where we can win.

That basic drift from the material and the concrete to the immaterial and symbolic is no accident. This is the constant dynamic in left politics because of a kind of elite capture. If you're a Black child living in poverty and neglect in the Brownsville neighborhood of Brooklyn, you might very well wonder how the annual controversy over the number of Black artists winning Oscars impacts your life. As much as you might want proportional representation (or perhaps greater than proportional representation) at awards shows, that kind of progress won't put food in your belly, shelter you from crime, or remove the lead that's poisoning you in your apartment. And yet our discourse on race politics fixates relentlessly on ephemeral and inconsequential cultural issues. Why?

Think again about that poor kid from Brownsville. While that kind of person is invoked constantly in left discourse, they don't *participate* in left discourse. They can't; they lack the cultural capital and economic stability to have a presence in our national media and politics. They quite literally cannot speak for themselves because they don't have forums or platforms that enjoy broad publicity. So the people who are left to speak for them are those among the most affluent and connected strata of American discourse. (The strata to which I belong.) Those who belong to marginalized groups who can take part in the national conversation are those within those groups who are the most well-connected, educated, and rich in cultural capital. This is particularly true of Black politicians, reporters, writers, pundits, and policymakers; they're typically dramatically more highly educated and more upwardly mobile than the average Black American. You can understand, then, why so much of the political energy in this country gets diverted into affective and symbolic issues: the people who talk about politics professionally, those who have the largest audiences, are in large majorities the people who face the least material depravation. In a similar dynamic to the long-standing trend that the poorest Americans don't vote, those who stand to benefit the most from muscular redistributive social policies are shut out from the conversation.

This dynamic reflects a broader failure of the left to remain true to its roots as a movement of the working class, of the poor, of the marginalized, of the dispossessed, of those at the bottom of the socioeconomic distribution. The American labor movement has been declining for longer than I've been alive, but it's essential to remember that in the first half of the twentieth century, labor unions and workers' parties won victory after victory: the weekend, the eight-hour workday and the forty-hour workweek, workplace health and safety protections, and robust collective bargaining rights. These victories were achieved not in spite of but because of the active participation and leadership of common workingmen. The movement had leaders, as all successful social movements must—the denial of leadership is a pathology of some left spaces that we will attend to in this book—but they were usually people like Eugene Debs, who was a great socialist intellectual but who had also worked on the railroads as a young man and thus had credibility among other workers.

Today, left-activist spaces are dominated by the college-educated, many of whom grew up in affluence and have never worked a day at a physically or emotionally demanding job. The inability to recruit from the working class and the uneducated has been a consistent source of frustration among leftist thinkers. Worse, there are now many in progressive spaces who decry the white working class—an immense group that still exerts heavy influence on American politics—as an inherently and permanently racist and bigoted class. This becomes a self-fulfilling prophecy, as left-leaning disdain for uneducated white workers and voters results in leftist cultural and communicative practices that seem tailor-made to reject the support of that large bloc. Left activists refuse to engage with the complexity of, for example, the millions of voters who supported Barack Obama in 2008 and 2012 but Donald Trump in 2016. This is, strategically, a kind of madness; any successful future for the left-of-center requires expanding our coalition and dreaming big when it comes to convincing disaffected lower-wage citizens to support us.

I strongly suspect that cultural issues are so dominant in many left spaces because culture is all the left feels like it controls. A common saw about current American politics is that the right has political power and craves cultural power, while the left has cultural power and craves political power. But with the disciplined and well-funded mainstream conservative movement using the inherently regressive elements of the American system (the Senate, the Electoral College, the Supreme Court) to ensure Republican dominance, it's just easier, emotionally and intellectually, to fixate on spaces like Hollywood, the news media, and academia, as these are the places where the left enjoys support bordering on hegemony. The trouble, of course, is that only power is power, and the left doesn't have it. I think so many leftists fixate on cultural and social issues to the detriment of economic and political power because they have simply given up on the latter.

It's fair to feel that the situation is bleak. The outsize demands of 2020, which spoke of fundamental changes in our basic civic structures, now appear fanciful. But hope is not lost. As much as I might prefer more tangible victories than the cultural ones the left has won in the recent past, cultural gains can be leveraged to gather more converts who might then help us create more tangible change. And despite the constant complaint of many leftists that the Democratic Party never improves (a species of the chronic pessimism that pervades the contemporary left), the policy platform of the Democratic Party in 2020 was far more progressive than that of 2008. Bernie Sanders lost in both 2016 and 2020 but expanded what millions of Americans thought of as politically possible. And our greatest strength lies in our current failure itself: the wealthy and corporations have gained such despotic control over our country's economy and political system that we have big, fat targets. Besides, unless you're planning to die anytime soon, there's nothing ever to do but keep going.

In the coming pages, I'll trace a brief history of how we got to the heady days of 2020. I'll connect that moment to previous eras that have been identified as politically fertile. I'll outline the differences between effective and ineffective left social movements, and I'll make the argument that we can revive the long-slumbering American workers' movement in a way that supports and amplifies the struggle of groups dedicated to racial justice, feminism, LGBTQ+ rights, and other marginalized populations. I'll spell out why a class-focused approach is appropriate not just for winning economic victories but for organizing around those identity issues as well. And I'll lay out concrete steps that individuals and groups can make today to ensure that their movements are more powerful.

The spirit of 2020 was always a righteous spirit, and the people and organizations that powered that moment had legitimate grievances and moral demands. Our inability to secure the better world that was promised should not distract us from the continued moral necessity of achieving it. What we need is practicality, resilience, and a plan. We have to get past thinking that our righteousness makes victory inevitable and start engaging in the real, tough, boring labor of convincing others. We have a lot of work to do, and there's no time like the present.

1

WHATEVER HAPPENED TO 2020?

One basic rule I try to follow when I write about current affairs is to remember that I do not live in extraordinary times. We live within the sweep of history, not outside of it, and it's our nature as conscious beings to assume that our times must be special because we live in them. But better to remember that today's crises will be little remembered.

And yet, in the summer of 2020, I found it hard to take my own advice. The Trump presidency had enflamed the country, his boorishness and serial scandals convincing many that the 2020 presidential election would prove to be one of the most consequential of our lifetimes. Along with sustained rage at Trump's long history of racist and misogynist statements, there was despair at his handling of the Covid-19 crisis. In March of that year, the virus had bloomed into a pandemic, spreading across our globalized world with unprecedented speed. In response to the crisis, state and city governments across the country had enforced lockdown policies that closed public spaces and kept people in their homes. Fear gripped the country as the virus killed hundreds of thousands, and being shut inside ratcheted up the tension. Trump was a focal point, but there was also enduring public anger about sexual misconduct in the workplace, systemic racism, and socioeconomic inequality. The #MeToo movement had galvanized public anger toward sexual misconduct, and the Bernie Sanders movement, with its army of newly minted socialists, continued to call for change through the Trump years. Our whole civic society seemed strewn with kindling. On May 25, 2020, four Minneapolis police officers lit the match.

The killing of George Floyd, an unarmed man accused of nothing more than passing a counterfeit bill, reverberated around the world. Covid-19 had devastated the economy, causing massive and immediate job losses of a kind rarely seen in American history. Floyd had recently lost jobs as a truck driver and a bouncer. In time, aggressive economic policies jump-started the American economy and led to historically low unemployment, but in May 2020, there was little comfort or support for an unemployed Black man. After a call from a store clerk, Minneapolis police officers arrived and detained Floyd. He was forced to the ground, and while there, one of the officers, Derek Chauvin, pressed his knee into Floyd's neck for nine minutes and twenty-nine seconds. By the time Chauvin released the hold, Floyd was dead. The video went viral, and the country exploded in protest.

Thanks to the multiplicative powers of the internet, Floyd's murder and the reaction to it are among the most discussed and analyzed events in human history. Yet I find that in spite of all the attention the 2020 political unrest provoked, there's a current of amnesia when it comes to that period. The heady, emotional, and radical atmosphere that predominated has evaporated. When we marched for justice, we chanted that things would never be the same. A few short years later, things very much look the same. People still speak about turning society upside down, but the fervor is gone, and many seem vaguely embarrassed to look back on it now.

To understand why, we need to go back and take stock of where we came from, of the political and cultural history that led us to what 2020 became.

PREHISTORY

I suspect that many remember the Obama administration with a kind of nostalgia. This is not merely a vestige of those who loved Obama and were satisfied by his administration—among whom I do not number—but also a yearning for a certain sense of normalcy. Pre-Trump normalcy. Where his successor brought chaos, Obama was always defined by his sense of composure and cool, which led members of his staff to nickname him "No Drama Obama." He also was blessed to stand in relief against his predecessor, George W. Bush, who had presided over 9/11, the quagmire in Afghanistan, the Iraq debacle, the horrors of the federal response to Hurricane Katrina, and the collapse of the American economy with the financial crisis and Great Recession. Obama's reign seemed to represent a return to something like normal.

But the association of the Obama administration with calming mundanity is a pretty cruel irony when you consider that he had taken office through a campaign based on hope and change. Business as usual is exactly the opposite of what candidate Obama had promised. I remember watching people make out in the park where Obama gave his victory address in 2008 and thinking that we had reached some sort of new era. It turned out that Obama would preside over a period of gridlock and little change, with his signature health care legislation representing the platonic ideal of compromise in American politics.

But during the 2008 campaign, a demand for change was in the air. The Great Recession and the financial crisis that spawned it were fresh on the minds of Americans, and particularly young Americans.

Millions of ambitious college students graduated into a brutal job market, which in turn depressed entry-level wages; despite the housing crash, the price of houses remained formidable, and the far more stringent lending requirements that followed the crisis put that core element of the American dream further out of reach. And no one could doubt who was responsible. In the history of economic crises, that of 2008 and 2009 was unique in how clearly it was the product of elite malfeasance. No one who paid attention to the facts of that situation could fail to understand that it was rich bankers who had tanked the economy and forced millions of Americans into financial ruin.

And yet despite this clear culpability, no accountability was forthcoming for the architects of the deepest recession since the Great Depression. The Obama administration refused to prosecute the bankers who had placed the economy in such dire straits in the pursuit of profit. Notoriously, only one senior banker was ever directly jailed for playing a role in the crisis. Worse, despite intense pressure from progressives, the Obama administration did essentially nothing for ordinary mortgage holders who suddenly found themselves facing foreclosure. For the first two years of the Obama administration, Democrats enjoyed the trifecta of federal government—holding the House, Senate, and presidency—yet offered no real relief. This lack of action for ordinary people looked particularly cruel in the shadow of the hundreds of billions of dollars that were spent bailing out the very banks that had created the crisis.

Obama inherited the recession and all of its problems from Bush. But his administration's failure to enact a genuinely progressive response to the crisis—by punishing the rich people who had caused it and by helping the poor people who suffered under it—would prove to be a bellwether for his two terms in office. To the immense frustration of many of those who had voted for him, the soaring vision of hope and change that he had sold to the public on the campaign trail led to a cautious and risk-averse presidency. Obama was almost maniacally interested in being the most reasonable person in the room, rather than in ruthlessly implementing a legislative agenda. This was an even more misguided way to lead after the 2010 midterm elections, when Obama was saddled with a permanently obstructionist Republican Congress that cared not at all about appearing reasonable. Ultimately, Obama ran as a transformative candidate and governed as an incrementalist president. As Andrew Sullivan wrote in 2017, approvingly, "Obama, in fact, was the conservative [during his administration]—nudging and amending, shaping and finessing as American society evolved—while the GOP flamed out in a reactionary dead end." It's fair to ask whether the millions of young liberals who had twice voted for Obama deserved more than another conservative presidency, however reasonable.

As the Obama presidency advanced, it became fashionable among more moderate-leaning Democrats to insist that he had never really been much of a radical and that those of us who demanded more from him had projected our politics onto him. But one need only look at the rhetoric with which Obama was sold to the nation to refute this. You can't hang the words "hope and change" on everything your candidate says and does and not expect people to demand hope and change from his presidency. The beatific images of Obama's face that became a campaign trail cliché spoke to the cult of personality that Democrats generated around their candidate. As Perry Bacon Jr. wrote in 2016, looking back at the administration as it neared its end, "Barack Obama ran for and entered the White House with the promise of becoming a transformational leader—someone who could alter the fundamental direction of the nation's politics in a more progressive way." Eight years of mostly business as usual disillusioned many who had rallied to his cause.

Exacerbating such tensions were generational politics, driven by the difficult financial fortunes of the youngest adults. During the Obama administration, millennials came of age—and they got screwed. They were entering into their prime wage-earning years and were barely scraping by. The employment depression that had been sparked by the financial crisis ruined their job prospects. Those who did have jobs saw their pay depressed by the slack labor market; there were always other people who would be willing to work for less. And the slowly building college-debt crisis hit them particularly hard. Untold thousands of young people were graduating from college in the Obama administration, having taken on tens of thousands of dollars in debt and finding their dream jobs totally unattainable. Given this history, and with hindsight, Occupy Wall Street seems like an inevitability.

In September 2011, with the unemployment rate still nearly twice that of what it had been in 2007, a ragtag group of protestors and activists occupied Zuccotti Park in New York's Financial District, the epicenter of the 2008 collapse. While the occupation in Zuccotti Park is frequently represented as spontaneous, various activists and groups had taken part in planning the action for months prior, and, in fact, the police had sufficient warning to block off two other potential sites for the protests. On the seventeenth, perhaps two hundred protesters decamped to the park, shouting and holding signs and making music as they arrived. They took over the park—they occupied Wall Street—and in so doing created a spectacle of resistance that attracted the attention of a country that was simmering with resentment toward the financial industry.

The protesters were an eclectic bunch, drawn from all manner of organizations and groups rather than from any one in particular. They spoke of a broken and rigged economy, a system designed to enrich the rich while leaving the rest of us behind. It was at Occupy that the "We Are the 99 Percent" slogan was first given national attention, meaning the bottom 99 percent of the income distribution, whose interests (said the protesters) were inherently antagonistic to the richest 1 percent. The slogan neatly captured the class dynamics that the protesters gathered to decry. Another slogan was popularized there, a much less widely publicized slogan but one with admirable style: "Shit Is Fucked Up and Bullshit." Such rhetoric is common when the entire system is being indicted.

To supporters, Occupy was a symbol of principled resistance, of people fed up with a rigged game; to detractors, it looked like a leftist stereotype, with all those crazy longhairs playing drums and muttering slogans. There was a great deal of music, poetry, and art at the occupation site, and many protesters had treated the occupation as an opportunity to express themselves on their pet issues. Topics like women's rights, freeing Palestine, and veganism were somewhat awkwardly bolted onto the action. The protesters in Zuccotti Park were passionate, but their message discipline was, it's fair to say, a little lacking.

Occupy generated a great mass of media attention and inspired many ancillary protests around the country. For some two months, the protesters defied increasing pressure from the city and police to disband, until finally the NYPD stormed the park in mid-November. From the vantage of history, we can say that Occupy Wall Street was a noble failure. Zuccotti Park galvanized many budding young leftists and for years after would be invoked as a turning point, but the event itself was brief. Writing this today, more than a decade after the initial protests, it's hard to find any concrete consequences of the movement. Occupy suffered from a few obvious weaknesses that ensured the movement would have little immediate effect. The two biggest are deeply entwined: the inability or refusal to generate coherent demands, and the addiction to intensely non-hierarchical—"horizontal"—decision-making.

The refusal of Occupy protesters to generate a list of specific demands became notorious. The headline of a *New York Times* story on the subject sums it up well: "Protesters Debate What Demands, if Any, to Make." Everyone involved knew that, in some way and to some degree, what they were protesting against was the basic economic compact of post-1980 America, a reality marred by vast socioeconomic inequality and labor insecurity caused directly by the greed and risk-taking of wealthy financiers. But no specific alternatives to the status quo were ever explicitly endorsed by Occupy Wall Street as an entity. To some extent, this was the result of the typical infighting and squabbling over priorities that are endemic to left movement building. But another major reason for the lack of specific demands is that some in Zuccotti Park were opposed to the very idea of specific demands. The *New York Times* piece I mentioned quoted a protester as saying, "Demands are disempowering since they require someone else to respond." This is a remarkable exercise in logic; a lack of demands is also disempowering, since without demands no one else has to respond. But that attitude appears to have been widespread. A friend of mine who attended the occupation for a week said that one protester had told him that "demands are hegemonic."

Absent demands, there's no sense of what a given protest or action intends to *do*. You might consider demands for most left actions to be essentially symbolic; certainly, when I was helping plan anti–Iraq War protests, no one thought that the government would really listen to our cry to bring the troops home. But demands serve an essential purpose even when they are very unlikely to be met in the short term. Building a movement is like rolling a small ball of snow down a hill so that it gathers more and more size over time. Every individual inch you gain adds very little to the ball, but over a long enough period of time the ball can grow large enough to knock your enemies down. This is how American social movements like temperance, abolitionism, or the labor agitation of the early twentieth century functioned. The trick is that you have to point the snowball at its target from the top of the hill; it's a very bad idea to try to steer the ball while it's already rolling downhill. Thanks to a not-entirely-hostile media—owing to the glaringly obvious fact that Wall

Street had devastated the country—Occupy was able to get a pretty good ball of snow rolling down the hill. But nobody, including the protesters themselves, seemed to have any idea where it was heading.

This resistance to developing a coherent lack of demands was emblematic of a larger problem with Occupy and, indeed, left organizing in general: the dedication to "horizontal" organization, the denial of leadership, the addiction to structurelessness. Occupy Wall Street operated purely through the vehicle of a general assembly, which is to say, a direct democracy system where everyone physically present was theoretically able to steer the group, regardless of their history with the group, amount of effort they had invested in it, or their experience with organizing. Occupy had no president, no executive committee, no officers, no leadership structure at all. There were committees, including a committee dedicated to proposing demands, but they had no real power and no greater ability to influence the debate than any other group of people.

There's a certain beauty to this kind of structurelessness, but it's also naive and counterproductive. Let's define the problem as simply as possible: the enemy enjoys the benefit of structure, and so we should too. Groups without any formal structure inevitably are dragged down by their least-productive members. I remember my frustration attending antiwar meetings in my early twenties when people who worked diligently for hours and hours every week were being shouted down by those who showed up to a meeting a couple of times a month and did little else. Leadership structures are common to human organizations for a reason; without leadership, endless time is wasted, groups are directionless and unfocused, and there's no accountability.

This is not a new problem! Activist groups in the 1960s and '70s were subject to this exact same problem. In 1972, the second-wave feminist and civil rights activist Jo Freeman published her classic article "The Tyranny of Structurelessness." In it, she meticulously described why horizontal

organizing is a mistake. In addition to the difficulty that leaderless organizations have in actually getting things done, Freeman pointed out that
this supposed lack of leadership inevitably papers over actually existing
differences in power within any given organization. "Contrary to what
we would like to believe, there is no such thing as a structureless group,"
she wrote, going on to point out that any group that calls itself leaderless actually has a de facto leadership class. Some organizers are more
engaged than others; some organizers are more dedicated than others;
some organizers are more influential and popular than others. These
differences will inevitably assert themselves in a given organization, no
matter how committed it might ostensibly be to denying leadership. As
Freeman wrote, "The very fact that we are individuals, with different
talents, predispositions, and backgrounds makes this inevitable." Perversely, the superficial denial of leadership can make power dynamics
in a given group more unhealthy. If someone in a group has the title of
president and acts in a way contrary to the group's best interest, a frank
conversation about their leadership can be had and, potentially, new
leaders can be chosen. In a nominally structureless organization, there
will be no formal means through which the most influential members
lose power. Thus ostensible leaderlessness strengthens the hand of those
who lead in reality if not in name.

When I was an undergraduate, I became a part of my college's Progressive Student Alliance (PSA). Those were heady days for me. I had
done my minor agitation in favor of gay rights in my teen years, and I was
at the time engaged in a Marxist reading group and diligently pursuing
a lefty self-education, but my desire to engage in organizing was at that
point still unfulfilled. PSA gave me my first vehicle for real activism. I
learned that organizing is often boring and a kind of mundane unpaid
labor, but also that personal relationships and social dynamics were as
important as political theory. I still look back at that time with fondness.

Our group had a lot of the problems that are common to left groups. We had splinter groups, secret meetings, red-baiting, and more. The role of the faculty adviser, a prominent political artist who had himself been a dedicated campus organizer in the tumultuous 1960s, was constantly controversial, with some members of our group accusing others of being his lackeys. We had frequent debates about how we needed to "really do something," with no clarity about what really doing something might entail. And yet at the core of everything, the group did good work. We held demos at school and elsewhere, invited groups to campus to talk, and organized trips to demonstrations in other states. But then came the consensus debate.

Like most organizations, the PSA had always been run according to conventional democracy. That is to say, issues would come up in meetings, we would vote, and the majority position would be declared the winner. We had officers, as required by the college, but no one took them too seriously. Voting, on the other hand, was the process through which we made decisions. Some of the members of the organizations had become convinced that voting was (here comes that word again) hegemonic. Voting, the claim went, forced those who disagreed to go along with the majority's whims. (Which is true; that's literally what voting is.) Rather than perpetuate this tyranny of the majority, we were to switch to a consensus decision-making system—if any member of the group disagreed with a given proposal, we could not proceed with it until that person was convinced. If they couldn't be convinced, we abandoned the proposal. Total unanimity would rule. That, I was told, was the only way to honor everyone's point of view.

I thought this was nuts, and I said so. Internal disagreement, I felt, was a central element of any healthy political group. Voting enabled individuals to register their disagreement and the group to move forward. Any organization that had pretenses to diversity should expect diversity of opinion. And frankly, consensus struck me as totalitarian; it was creepy to imagine a world where everyone agreed all the time. Give me dissent in all things.

Most members of the group wanted to adopt a consensus-based decision-making process. So I said, "Let's take the vote"; I was prepared to lose and move on. But others in the group insisted that this was not good enough. To adopt consensus, they said, we had to arrive at consensus. There had to be unanimity on the decision of whether to require unanimity in the decision-making process. As I said at the time, this made no sense; we had a voting-based system in place, and we could only change to a different system through the old one. But I was shouted down. We had to have consensus on the question of consensus.

When the day arrived to decide on our decision-making process, I was the one person who out-and-out rejected the consensus-based system, though some other people expressed misgivings. Everyone was asked whether they consented to consensus, and only I said no. We went around the table again and again, but I was firmly convinced that the move was a mistake. The meeting was rancorous and uncomfortable and ended with no resolution. The following week, I was approached privately by two members of the group. They told me that I was obstructing the group and an impediment to change. They told me that I shouldn't return, so I never did. I hope the irony isn't lost on you: a change to our decision-making process that was explicitly endorsed as a way to "honor" dissenting voices had resulted in my expulsion from the group because I dissented.

There's a funhouse-mirror quality of structureless organizations. They're meant to remove power imbalances, but they inevitably result in power imbalances of a more toxic kind. Occupy suffered from precisely this ugly dynamic, and the tangled animosities of Zuccotti Park are legendary among left organizers.

Occupy Wall Street exploded and then fizzled for a lot of reasons, the biggest of which is that its members were opposing the American financial industry and the state forces that defend it. Victory was never in the cards. And yet for all of that, it remains a deeply influential piece of American history and proved to be a harbinger of things to come. Post–Zuccotti Park, the language and symbols of American politics were never the same. What happened in the years that followed was in the spirit of Occupy—and the shadow of the terrible recession. Occupy Wall Street was the beginning of a flowering of socialist messaging and thought.

It may be hard for younger readers to understand how deeply things have changed. When I first started blogging in 2008, the American left—the left-of-liberal left, the radical left, the socialist left—had been almost entirely written out of the public debate. Some stalwart radical publications and writers endured, but the socialist left was considered by most in the mainstream media to be anachronistic and moribund. The default left-of-center voice was not a socialist or radical but rather a technocratic liberal, writers in the mold of Jonathan Chait and Matthew Yglesias, loyal Democrats who tacitly or explicitly accepted the Clintonian vision of neo-liberal politics, the "the era of big government is over" kind. Publications like the *New Republic* reflexively dismissed any political engagement more radical than the default center-left position. The *New York Times* and the *Washington Post* carefully defined the boundaries of the *very serious*, and socialists weren't within them. Stung by years of Republicans representing all Democrats as out-of-touch crazies, and beholden to a wealthy donor class that was friendly to social progressivism but resistant to higher taxes, the organizations that made up the country's liberals routinely dismissed anyone demanding genuinely left-wing change.

Occupy helped to change that. Resistance to George W. Bush's presidency had grown steadily during his terms. But John Kerry, his 2004 campaign opponent, was as much of an establishment Democrat as you can imagine, and most of the rhetoric of that period was no more radical than whatever Jon Stewart was saying each night on *The Daily Show*. The financial crisis helped to thaw the ice around the American left. Unrest had been bubbling up for years after the recession gripped America, but Occupy focused it, rallying support for America's restive radicals and helping to improve the visibility of left-of-liberal politics. There was a flowering of socialist essays and publications. *Jacobin* magazine, a (more-or-less) explicitly Marxist journal, had been founded a year before, and had its profile significantly boosted by the Occupy moment, as did the *New Inquiry*, founded in 2009. Both publications captured the rage of those who felt conned by America's meritocratic system, people who had diligently worked in high school and graduated from college and found themselves in a punishing job market.

Still, the national political scene remained largely unchanged. Obama met the 2012 challenge of Mormon former governor Mitt Romney's Republican campaign for president with his usual placid demeanor, and despite briefly trailing in the polls during the election, he ultimately won a comfortable victory in the Electoral College. He remained stymied in Congress. The conservative base had been energized by the Tea Party movement, a collection of "patriots" who protested big government and high taxes—though American taxes were not particularly high in that period, in historical terms. The Tea Party was subject to repeated accusations of being astroturf, which is to say, a fake grassroots movement actually powered by well-moneyed conservative forces. True or not, the Tea Party demonstrated the continued salience of movement conservatism; the right-wing American Enterprise Institute estimated that some 10 percent of the American public supported the Tea Party movement, and it certainly dwarfed the number of Americans who supported Occupy. Liberal critics of the Tea Party argued that it was powered by racism toward America's first Black president.

Obama's second term was dogged by a near-total refusal of cooperation from congressional Republicans. Without congressional majorities, the Obama administration was forced to nibble around the edges to enact change. There were some advances in this period, but it's telling that the most prominent of them, the federal legalization of gay marriage, was the result of a Supreme Court decision and not of legislation. Increasingly emboldened left-wing critics hit Obama for his incrementalist approach, his continued refusal to prosecute bankers responsible for the financial crisis, and the secretive drone war that was killing civilians in Afghanistan and Pakistan. It seemed clear that the Democratic Party was facing a reckoning over its future direction and its level of radicalism. The battleground was the 2016 Democratic primaries, pitting leftist outsider Bernie Sanders against centrist insider Hillary Clinton.

Hillary Clinton burst into public life during her husband's presidency. Unusually accomplished and well-credentialed for a First Lady, Clinton had used the spotlight aggressively. She was a key influence on the Clinton administration's failed effort to remake the American health care system. She published books, stumped for Democrats, and happily inserted herself into public political controversies. All of this contributed to making her an object of obsession for many American conservatives, who were all too happy to insult her looks, her intelligence, and her character. There's no doubt that this negative attention was influenced by (and sometimes entirely the product of) a particularly vicious kind of sexism. It's also true that she was a uniquely divisive presence in American politics, with some of the worst popularity metrics in American political history. Despite that, after her husband's term ended, she became a senator for New York and then ran for the presidency in 2008, famously losing to the upstart Obama despite her initial frontrunner status.

In 2015, having added a stint as Obama's secretary of state to her experience, Clinton declared her candidacy for Democratic nominee for the presidency. Clinton could hardly have been more of an insider, a paid-up member of the Democratic establishment running with the blessings of a sitting president. Clinton also benefited from the perception that it was "her turn," especially given her failed attempt to capture her party's nomination in 2008. Her nomination was seen as inevitable.

That sense of inevitability was challenged from a truly unexpected direction. Bernie Sanders, a senator from Vermont and officially an Independent, ran against Clinton and attracted a shocking level of support in doing so. He had a proud history as a local lefty and activist, but his service in the Senate had been fairly undistinguished, having failed to champion any particularly meaningful legislation. A battle between the consummate Democratic insider and a then little-known senator from one of the country's smallest states would not seem to be a fair fight. And, indeed, Clinton would go on to win fairly handily. But not before Sanders changed American politics.

Sanders was able to win several states in a primary campaign that was considered a fait accompli, for several reasons. For one, he took advantage of Clinton's unpopularity. Clinton's status as the anointed choice of the Democratic establishment could not counter the fact that so many voters had a negative opinion about her and were angry at party leadership. Sanders's shocking win in Michigan underlined how many voters were disillusioned with the establishment of the party, which had presided over decades of decline in industry and manufacturing that had devastated the local economy. Clinton's husband had embraced globalization with the North American Free Trade Agreement (NAFTA), which many blamed for job losses and shuttered factories. Throughout the primary, Sanders benefited from simmering resentment over the perception that the Democrats had become a party of elites.

As an avowed democratic socialist, Sanders enjoyed considerable credibility with voters who demanded the type of revolutionary change the Democrats were unwilling to pursue. The Occupy generation had a new flag to rally around. The frustration and anger that had bubbled along since the financial crisis found the perfect vehicle for expression. The seventy-five-year-old Sanders became the candidate of the youth, and millions of dollars in small donations flowed into his campaign. A sophisticated online outreach apparatus was built to raise both money and awareness, and later campaigns would look on it as a model for outreach.

Sanders would lose the 2016 primary. Clinton was too well-established, had too much institutional backing, and benefited too much from some of the strange antidemocratic systems of the Democratic primary rules, such as the superdelegate system. Ultimately though, it would be unfair to suggest that Clinton won only because of dirty tricks. The fact of the matter is that she was able to rally more voters than Sanders, who in particular struggled to attract the moderate Black voters who many see as the heart of the party. But the Sanders moment would prove lasting and consequential. Finally, there was a left-wing champion within the party who could stand against the centrist instincts of so many in Washington. What had been dismissed as a dead religion for so long had risen again.

A good indicator of the return of socialism to relevance can be found in the growth of the Democratic Socialists of America (DSA). A legacy organization borne from some classic leftist infighting in the 1970s, the DSA saw a sharp uptick in membership during Sanders's run for the presidency. The organization tripled in membership size between early 2016 and early 2017.

The evolution of DSA serves as an object lesson in the drift of the left-of-center over the past few decades. As someone raised in a communist household, I had always resented DSA, which was founded to be the anti-communist socialist organization. DSA members were forever denouncing communist states and their various abuses; I thought of them as people who fell all over themselves to reassure you that they were not the wrong kind of radical, to the detriment of actually achieving radical ends. Yet when I talk to people about DSA now, they have no idea that DSA was once well-known as the conservative socialist institution. And, of course, most of the new generation of socialists were not even born when the Soviet Union fell.

Complicating everything was the absurd and destructive presidency of Donald Trump. His ascension to the position of leader of the Republican Party, and his subsequent presidential administration, still feels fake somehow. Everything about it was so bizarre that it's hard for me to believe that it was real. But real it was, and we're living with the consequences. Taking advantage of a Republican Party that lacked a clear leader at the end of the Obama administration, and leveraging his considerable celebrity for attention, Trump bullied his way to the Republican nomination, ridiculing his primary opponents and breaking every unwritten rule and taboo of conventional politics. Greedy for ratings, the cable news networks discussed Trump relentlessly, giving him immense amounts of free publicity and helping to establish him as a serious candidate in the minds of the Republican electorate. For months, political analysts denied that he had a chance at the nomination. Meanwhile, he kept winning.

The rest is history. Trump eked out an Electoral College victory against Clinton in November 2016, despite losing the popular vote. Her abundant vulnerabilities had come back to haunt the party. The Democrats had nominated one of the least popular politicians in public polling history as their candidate for the most important political office in the world. Trump cleaned up in areas of the country that had been devastated by deindustrialization and job loss, including in Michigan and Wisconsin—two pivotal states where Clinton barely campaigned. The Clinton campaign's focus on celebrity glitz and glamour seemed like a bad fit with a country that was still experiencing economic instability. We had spent a year hearing people declare "I'm with Her." It turned out that most of the country was not.

Supporters of Sanders saw Clinton's loss as confirmation of their critique of the establishment Democratic Party: that it had become a party of elites, ruled by overeducated members of the professional class, unable to connect with parts of the country that suffered from economic devastation. But many liberals quickly decided that Clinton's loss was straightforwardly a consequence of racism and argued that critiquing the Democrats for their abandonment of the working class amounted to sympathy for bigots. That so many were willing to chalk up a white woman's electoral failures to racism tells you something about the rhetorical environment in contemporary liberalism.

Trump's presidency amounted to a steady parade of gaffes and crises. Trump found it difficult to enact a legislative agenda: he failed to meaningfully change policy on his campaign's signature issue of immigration, his Obamacare repeal effort failed to get past members of Congress in his own party, and the only major legislation he successfully passed was a large tax cut for the wealthy and corporations, hardly in keeping with the populist feints he had deployed on the campaign trail. That Republicans could force through tax cuts and no other major bills tells you something about the nature of American democracy.

Trump's presidency, as destructive as it was, instilled American politics with a sense of the absurd. His various efforts to restrict immigration and crack down on undocumented immigrants who were already here had a high human cost, as did other aspects of his presidency. But it was hard not to see the farcical elements of his reign; the daily scandals, resignations, and missteps created a grimly comic atmosphere.

One element of Trump's persona was always treated deathly seriously. Near the end of the 2016 election cycle, a video emerged of Trump bragging to a television host about his tendency to aggressively pursue women, even the unwilling, notoriously saying that he would "grab them by the pussy," presuming his celebrity made him entitled to sexual gratification. At the time of the video's release, it was thought that it might be an insurmountable political hurdle. It wasn't, but about a year later, the issue of sexual entitlement and misconduct burst into the public consciousness again.

In November 2017, the *New York Times* published an investigation into the serial sexual aggression of the movie producer Harvey Weinstein, provoking immense public reaction. Other victims of Weinstein came forward, and their sheer number was shocking. In the days that followed, more and more people stepped forward to allege sexual misconduct, first in Hollywood and later in all manner of other fields. Social media amplified these accusations. Simmering anger over Trump's infamous comments about assaulting women finally boiled over. In time, activists, accusers, and allies rallied around a hashtag to give their efforts a name: #MeToo.

The Trump administration was forever dogged by petty scandals, and members of the administration came and went with comical regularity, most of which were low-stakes, mere embarrassments. But toward the end of his tenure, the United States was engulfed in a singular crisis. The Covid pandemic had its genesis in 2019 (thus Covid-*19*), but bloomed into a full-blown global emergency in March 2020. As large-scale lockdowns were established in the United States, it became clear to many Americans that their basic way of life would be deeply disrupted. Being forced to stay home for long periods made an already internet-addicted country turn even more deeply into its smartphones. Mask mandates and social-distancing guidelines made rare trips outside, such as to get groceries, into tense affairs. Fairly early in the pandemic, it would be conclusively proven that outdoor transmission of the virus was extremely unlikely, but for some months most people masked outdoors and would often take a wide path around others as they walked by. The national mood was as tense as I've ever experienced. And the Trump administration's perceived blunders at the beginning of the crisis amplified an already heightened partisan atmosphere. The country felt like it was on the brink of something; there was a sense that the center could not hold.

Those were the conditions that primed the country for an explosion, one that was triggered by the murder of George Floyd in May 2020.

THE SIMMER BOILS OVER

Floyd's brutal execution became one of the most viral events in the history of politics. (Imagine if Emmett Till had been killed in the era of smartphone cameras and social media.) Protests broke out in hundreds of American cities, with some seeing marches and unrest every day for months. It was estimated that, in terms of combined count of participants across the country, the protests were the largest in US history. The protests were predominantly peaceful, but riots did break out in some cities, notably Chicago and Portland. In Seattle, an anarchist "autonomous zone" was carved out for many weeks, with police and city government essentially ceding control of the area. Already charged, the political climate reached a level of fervor I had never previously experienced. On social media, the conversation raged, brought to a fever pitch by the perceived stakes of ending white supremacy.

It was not merely Black Americans who were considered targets. The Stop Asian Hate movement cried out against aggression and violence against Asian Americans. A string of high-profile attacks on innocent Asian citizens prompted months of condemnation in journalism and on social media. The origins of Covid-19 in China, and the fear that these origins would result in anti-Asian reprisals, were much discussed. Reports were put out detailing hate crimes against Asian victims. Hard data demonstrating a wave of anti-Asian violence was difficult to come by, but the many individual attacks, some of them on video, contributed to a culture of fear. Adding to the already discussed tensions that were ripping the country apart, Stop Asian Hate helped to underline that Americans from all sorts of backgrounds found the contemporary United States an inhospitable, often violent place, and contributed to a tense and combative atmosphere.

These immense stores of political passion often found expression in misguided attacks on those who stepped out of line. In late May, just days after Floyd's death, the Democratic data analyst David Shor tweeted a political science paper that argued that the riots that followed the assassination of Martin Luther King Jr. had swayed voters and helped elect Richard Nixon. The argument was that of the academics who had written the paper, and Shor accurately summarized its conclusions, but these facts did little to change the reaction to his tweets. The response was immediate and harsh, with thousands of Twitter users attacking Shor, arguing that by tweeting the paper he was implicitly criticizing the BLM movement. That Black Lives Matter was not to be criticized was simply assumed. One enterprising person shared Shor's tweet with his employer, Civis Analytics, and a few days later he was gone. To add a little more absurdity to the scenario, Shor was also kicked out of a LISTSERV called Progressphiles—which Shor had not posted on in more than two years.

Those who raised concerns about Shor were frequently accused of false equivalence, of suggesting that the treatment of Shor was "as bad" as the racism that the protestors fought against. That no one was actually arguing that went unnoticed. As Jonathan Chait of *New York* magazine wrote of the imbroglio, "it is an error to jump from the fact that right-wing authoritarian racism is far more important to the conclusion that left-wing illiberalism is completely unimportant."

The Shor affair appears to me an almost custom-made object lesson in the left's destructive resistance to internal debate. Shor's tweets were about tactics, not a disagreement about goals; he said nothing that indicated that he was anything less than dedicated to the cause of fighting racial inequality. Instead, he pointed to the work of an academic—a Black academic, as it happens—whose research had shown that nonviolent protest was more likely to result in progressive outcomes than riots. That stance is certainly fair game for criticism and disagreement. But the reaction was absurd. More than absurd: it was directly counterproductive to the cause that Shor's critics thought they were defending. Internal criticism and tactical disagreements don't weaken a movement; they do the opposite. Like a vaccine provokes immunity to disease, internal dissent within a movement helps to make it stronger against attack. How can the basic work of deciding what is to be done and how to do it survive in a rhetorical atmosphere in which saying the wrong thing might result in the loss of your livelihood?

This was the poisonous atmosphere that developed in left political spaces in the summer of 2020. Few wanted to step out of line and speak up about the oppressive discursive conditions. The nail that sticks up, as the saying goes, gets hammered down. (During that period, I enjoyed an essential form of protection: I don't have a Twitter account.) The treatment of Shor, and a similar controversy regarding the journalist Lee Fang, who had also been engulfed in controversy following tweets seen as critical of BLM, helped to establish a basic element of the 2020 moment: fear. Fear of stepping out of line. Fear of criticizing "the movement." Fear of being perceived to be on the wrong side. The dynamic that defined 2020 was a culture of self-censorship. I will always remember that year as a time when so many people, including those who trafficked in opinions for a living, felt compelled to keep their heads down, unwilling to make waves and risk the wrath of the crowd.

Meanwhile, the media's increasingly activist rhetoric became hard to ignore. It's long been observed that members of the mainstream media (that is to say, neither explicitly right- or left-wing) are dominantly left-leaning and Democratic. The degree of this dominance, and the extent to which it influences coverage, are fiercely controversial. Endless books have been written to hash out the degree of a "liberal bias" in media. Broadly speaking, I do believe there's a liberal bias in media—and also a corporatist bias, a nationalist bias, an establishment bias. But in the summer of 2020, the conversation within media about its biases evolved. Galvanized by the post-Floyd atmosphere, many reporters and pundits seemed to shed any pretense to neutrality and began discussing their work straightforwardly as a kind of activism.

Some were ready to question the pretense of journalistic objectivity altogether. In a widely read and influential *New York Times* opinion piece, Wesley Lowery wrote that the media should modify its pretenses to neutrality and embrace a "moral clarity" that had developed in light of the George Floyd killing. "For years, I've been among a chorus of mainstream journalists who have called for our industry to abandon the appearance of objectivity as the aspirational journalistic standard," wrote Lowery, reflecting on broad trends in his industry. Lowery's essay, appearing prominently in the *New York Times*—the closest thing we have to the official voice of the journalism industry—was broadly received as a cri de coeur over the future of the media. Though Lowery's essay was more nuanced and complex than its reputation, many journalists and pundits accepted as given the suggestion that the industry was leaving behind the concept of objectivity or neutrality and celebrated that development. For Lowery, one specific example of a more honest sphere of legitimate controversy was one that excluded debate on whether Trump was a racist; he simply was, wrote Lowery, and a media that embraced the "moral clarity" Lowery championed was one that would permit no disagreement about that fact.

It happens that I do think Donald Trump is a racist. I also think it's clear that American policing has been systematically brutal to people of color, and that the history of police violence against Black people is a series of horrors. We desperately need serious police reform to address these awful killings. We also need to understand that the shootings are one element of a broader reality of policing, with selective enforcement, intimidation, and racial profiling being daily elements of Black life in America. But the reductive simplicity of the "moral clarity" argument—or, at least, the social media version that removed the complexity and qualification of Lowery's essay—makes us less able to confront these problems intelligently, not more. To insist that some journalists are now in possession of moral clarity, and that we have no particular responsibility to trouble that simplicity, narrows the range of acceptable opinion and prevents us from understanding the best way forward.

Take, for example, the fact that in total numbers (but not in terms of rate or percentage) the police kill more white Americans than Black. This is the kind of fact that was not within "the sphere of legitimate controversy" among progressives in 2020. As the conversation about police brutality against Black men took over our entire political discourse, it became a matter of rigid doctrine that no one was to talk about the fact that far more Black men were killed by other Black men than by police. And there's a strong logic to this: conservatives use the existence of violence within the Black community as a way to distract from the sins of violent cops. As the activist Mansfield Frazier wrote of the reaction to the 2012 killing of teenager Trayvon Martin, outrage about which presaged the Black Lives Matter movement, "The killing of Trayvon Martin has focused the attention of conservatives on the high rate of homicides in urban communities, but only as a means of deflecting attention away from George Zimmerman." But the conversation must allow for nuance, and nuance was in short supply in the heated days of 2020. I will discuss these issues in the next chapter. For now, it's enough to say that a rigid sense of acceptable opinion developed among progressives—no opinion more acceptable than the quixotic quest to defund the police.

DEMANDS ARE ASSEMBLED

The idea of defunding the police has already attracted more debate than I can summarize, and I will deal with it in more depth later. For now, it's sufficient to say that through the tangled and chancy process through which broad social movements operate, defunding the police became the central demand of the Black Lives Matter protests. Protests still simmered across the country, sometimes in defiance of Covid lockdowns. It had become clear by midsummer that some kind of central demand was necessary for the movement to make progress. "Defund the police" was, at least, an effective sound bite. Unfortunately, there was little consensus about what exactly it meant. Some insisted that the purpose of Defund was not to shutter police departments entirely but rather to reallocate some police resources to other agencies and purposes. The people who held this view frequently insisted that no one was calling for literal police abolition. Unfortunately for them, in June, the *New York Times* ran an opinion piece by Mariame Kaba titled "Yes, We Mean Literally Abolish the Police." The actual merits of defunding the police aside, the fundamental confusion about what was being demanded blunted the force of Black Lives Matter despite its unprecedented media attention and public support. Besides, however intensely the protests had captivated the American public, abolishing the police or drastically defunding them, at large scale, was simply never in the cards.

More granular reforms were proposed. Some of these demands coalesced into the George Floyd Justice in Policing Act, which among other things would have expanded the federal government's oversight over potentially racist police departments, provided funding for investigations into police misconduct, and created a national registry for police violence. There were activists who saw the bill as a watered-down compromise, and many protesters still called for a total reform of the American system.

But the bill at least crystalized many of the commonsense reforms that were available to be made; it may have been low-hanging fruit, but such fruit still deserves to be picked. Unfortunately, while the bill passed the House of Representatives on a party-line vote in 2021, it died in the Senate. Democrats vowed to keep working, but in the years since, very little of substance has emerged. On the other side of the aisle, Black Republican senator (and rising GOP star) Tim Scott proposed his own policing-reform bill, which focused on improved record keeping, increased penalties for filing false police reports, banning chokeholds, and increasing the use of police body cameras. But that bill too died in the legislature.

This failure to achieve material change legislatively was disappointing, though there were more successes on the local and state levels. Everywhere though, there was a sense that the amount of change accomplished was not matching the moment. A good example can be found in Minneapolis, the site of Floyd's murder, and the journey I mentioned earlier—the city council voted to dissolve their entire police force, which action was watered down until it amounted to only a modest reduction in police funds, before finally the city council voted to *increase* funding to their police force. This farcical element of a tragic story tells you quite a bit about how difficult it is to translate protest into power.

THE WAVE ROLLS BACK

By the end of 2020, the street protests had run out of steam. The ambient sense of fear and consequences online began to thaw. Eventually, Derek Chauvin would be found guilty of killing Floyd, with the other officers facing lesser legal consequences. This was an essential part of what had been demanded and a matter of absolute justice. But protesters had said from the beginning that what was needed was structural change, not individual accountability, and such change was hard to find.

The #MeToo movement had continued to bubble along in 2020, and that year saw some important milestones, such as the arrest of sex trafficker Ghislaine Maxwell (recently convicted and awaiting appeal) and the conviction of Harvey Weinstein, who was sentenced to decades in prison. More ominously, the legal machinations that would result in the trial between Johnny Depp and Amber Heard moved forward.

All of this happened against the backdrop of the singular tension and intensity of a presidential election. Donald Trump's first term was drawing to a close. A crowded Democratic primary field had produced at least a half dozen candidates viewed as viable. Among them was Bernie Sanders, who once again sketched out an alternative to Democratic establishment politics based on programs like Medicare for All, which would have radically shifted the financial burden of medicine off of the lower and middle classes and onto higher earners through higher taxes. Perhaps stung by the (baseless) accusations of sexism and racism that had dogged his primary fight with Hillary Clinton, Sanders took more care to use terminology from identity politics, underlining his commitment to social justice. The crowded field for the primary jostled against itself throughout 2019 and early 2020. No doubt influenced by the country's protest movements and resistance to Trump, the candidates largely tried to position themselves to the left. Particularly salient were issues of climate change and health care.

For months the candidates jockeyed against one another, with the field gradually winnowing. For a brief, energizing period, it appeared that Sanders was the front-runner. In February, he won the Nevada caucuses, a significant enough event that the *New York Times* suggested it "may make it difficult for the still-fractured moderate wing of the Democratic Party to slow his march to the nomination." With the threat of a truly leftist presidential candidate hovering, that fracturing was addressed by the ghost of the party's center-left past, Barack Obama. After Sanders's win in Nevada, a number of high-profile candidates dropped out of the race and threw their endorsements behind the establishment's choice, Joe Biden. It was widely reported in that period that Obama had worked behind the scenes to convince other candidates to drop out and support Biden. The champion of cautious liberal incrementalism seemed to have kneecapped the left wing of the party. After a campaign defined by jockeying to be perceived as the most progressive candidate, and despite much media rhetoric that the party was pushing left, the establishment's choice, a seventy-seven-year-old centrist, received the nomination.

This was not, incidentally, the first time Obama had played kingmaker in a way designed to attack the left. In 2016, after the grueling Clinton–Sanders primary fight, many saw Minnesota representative Keith Ellison's bid to head the Democratic National Committee as a chance for left-wing Democrats to enjoy a champion inside the party apparatus. There too, it is widely alleged, Obama used his influence to get a loyalist, Tom Perez, into the position.

The 2020 presidential campaign was a strange affair. The country had been on fire with protests for half a year, and Covid colored everything, with precautions against the virus preventing a good deal of the typical campaigning. Kissing babies had certainly taken on a new sense of danger. On the campaign trail, Trump's bizarre antics were pitted against Biden's perceived mental fogginess and his frequent difficulties when speaking. Polls had indicated a fairly easy victory for Biden, but when Election Day arrived, Biden sweated out a narrow one. The polls had underrated Trump's chances again, perhaps due to a refusal of Trump voters to answer their phones when pollsters called. Trump, infamously, refused to concede, called the election stolen before many of the states had even finished counting, and eventually whipped up the riot at the Capitol building on January 6, 2021.

That was the year that was 2020: a year of pandemic, a year of protest, a year of tension and turmoil, a year when the establishment of American politics regained the presidency, replacing the serial instability and alleged petty corruption of the Trump administration with Joe Biden's uninspiring, incrementalist normalcy.

The passion and discord that had dominated 2020 gave way, in the end, to the election of a consummate insider and establishment candidate. The protest movements would continue to influence American politics for years to come, but as 2020 ended it was clear that a particular moment had ended as well. The moderate candidate in the Democratic Party—the "adult in the room"—had prevailed, and the liberal party in US politics had demonstrated that in a year defined by radical foment, the incrementalists still ruled. Protestors still occasionally took to the streets. Black Lives Matter signs still hung in windows. Radical magazines still published articles outlining a radical future. But the sense of possibility that had filled the summer of 2020 had markedly dimmed.

There's no shame in failing to pull the system up by the roots. As a radical anti-capitalist, I'm used to losing; my political movement has done little else but lose for my entire lifetime. Change takes time. I'm all for revolution, but I know that history usually makes us wait. The problem with the revolutionary spirit of 2020 was not the desire for systemic change. Not in such a rotten system. The problem with 2020 was that activists and journalists and academics mistook heat for light. The George Floyd protests were some of the most well-publicized in human history, and it's true that publicity is necessary for a protest movement to succeed. But if the last few years proved anything, it's that publicity alone can't make change.

Could it have gone differently? More than anything, the revolutionary spirit of 2020 suffered from a lack of organization. The disparate threads of progressive dissatisfaction were never woven into a garment that could bear weight. I will discuss the particular organizational difficulties of

Black Lives Matter later in this volume. For now it's enough to say that, as billions of dollars poured in to support the cause, the lack of a central organization that ensured transparency and accountability meant that there was no clear direction for the movement to go. Without an organization, there was no vehicle for arriving at specific goals and working toward them. Many lists of demands were written, but no group had sufficient influence or authority to determine *the* demands. Meanwhile, an understandable desire to defer to Black Lives Matter left other progressive organizations in a kind of limbo. No left group would have been foolish enough to seek to be the umbrella organization under which #MeToo or BLM might fall. But without such an overarching organization, the various movements and causes that helped generate the spirit of limitless political possibility could not come together for real populist power.

Corporations published diversity statements. Universities updated their sexual misconduct guidelines. A veritable army of young idealists was hired into positions at nonprofit agencies. And a new spirit of social control descended onto social media. But the galvanizing events and radical energy of 2020 were squandered. Conservatives always have home field advantage in politics; they win when nothing happens. And more powerful than any conservative reaction was the ultimate enemy of a revolutionary moment: time. The passage of time pitilessly grinds away at progressive movements, sapping strength, dissipating political anger, undermining solidarity. People, good people, had demanded that the world stop in response to injustice. But the world never stops.

My views, and this entire book, will be taken as a harsh indictment of the people and groups that gathered together to demand change in 2020. And there are criticisms to be made if we are to better understand the way change happens and thus to ensure that it actually does. But there's no shame in failing to achieve radical change. Not in these United States, where the forces of reaction jealously hoard power. I will always have affection and respect for those who agitated for change in 2020, who took to the streets, who demanded a better world. The purpose of critical engagement with protest movements is to strengthen them, make them better, to create the conditions where the world they dreamed of can become a reality. And for all of my complaints, which I register from the comfort of history and with the benefit of hindsight, I too was taken with the spirit of possibility of what was a remarkable year.

In *Fear and Loathing in Las Vegas*, Hunter S. Thompson wrote his eulogy for the radical spirit of the '60s, calling that period "the crest of a high and beautiful wave." In the 1960s too it seemed for a time like the possibilities were endless. But as Thompson recognized, the inevitable happened, and "now, less than five years later, you can go up on a steep hill in Las Vegas and look West, and with the right kind of eyes you can almost see the high-water mark—that place where the wave finally broke and rolled back."

2

BPMCLM: BLACK LIVES MATTER AND THE INEVITABILITY OF ELITE CAPTURE

Race has been the third rail of American politics for generations. Even as a child in the 1980s, it was clear to me that race was something different, something more intense and dangerous, than all the rest of the stuff of politics. As I grew up, and American culture evolved, the politics of humanities departments at elite universities seeped out into the broader discourse and gradually conquered our institutions, and race grew to be something like the singular fulcrum on which political debate pivoted. In the past several years, racial discourse has grown only more heightened, and the communal diktat has been to consider the racial implications of everything, all the time.

American racism is a panoply of evils, great and small, and it has proven to be remarkably adaptable, a great survivor. The moral necessity of confronting it could not be more clear. The murder of George Floyd in May 2020 was both a sudden flashpoint and the culmination of years of frustration and rage. The unjustifiable killing of Black men is as old as the United States of America. Floyd's death harkened back to the era of lynchings and to the martyrs of the civil rights era. And it was no outlier. The 2012 killing of teenager Trayvon Martin, while not committed by a police officer, demonstrated the tendency for Black youth to be viewed as acceptable targets for surveillance and violence. The 2014 death of eighteen-year-old Michael Brown at the hands of a white police officer in Ferguson, Missouri, sparked mass protests and led to the birth of Black Lives Matter, a new radical protest movement that demanded major police reform and a broader reckoning over race in America. In the following years, a steady drip of prominent Black deaths at the hands of the police kept the fire burning, with names like Freddie Gray, Sandra Bland, and Tamir Rice added to the roster of those taken too soon thanks to the actions of the police. In time, the focus on police misconduct provoked renewed anger over other incidents, such as the March 2020 killing of Breonna Taylor, shot to death by police in Louisville while she lay in bed.

Covid and Trump had already made 2020 a year of tension and unease when a raw cell phone video of a group of Minneapolis police officers detaining, assaulting, and murdering George Floyd, an unarmed Black man, set the world on fire. It provoked an international response of unprecedented scale. Seemingly every corner of our culture responded to Floyd's death, and there was a wave of righteous anger over the ongoing brutalization of Black Americans. The forces of reaction, of course, found ways to dismiss and minimize what had happened, but to an unprecedented degree in a divided America, the institutions of civic life joined hands to condemn Floyd's killing and demand change. The trouble was, and remains, to define what change exactly, and to what end?

The protests that shook the country were just that, street protests, and it's not the job of street protesters to express perfectly clear and coherent political goals that could be taken up by our political system. Instead, they cried out for justice, change, a reckoning. Part of what made

2020 different, in theory, was that the institutions were listening—the media, the charitable foundations and nonprofits, our political parties, our courts, our legislature. Yet no one would look back today and suggest that enough was done. Indeed, in time, very understandable resentment has grown that so little changed. The post–George Floyd moment was indeed unprecedented, but it did not bring unprecedented change.

Black Lives Matter has both failed and been failed. It was a noble movement to defend the Black underclass; it was waged by members of a Black professional class whose interests and biases are not the same as that of the median Black voter. But to understand all of that, we need to start at the beginning.

VIOLENCE, POLICE AND NOT

Police violence is a particularly visible and particularly unsettling expression of racial inequality. But the day-to-day realities of racial difference are just as stark and much more widespread. In statistical terms, the status of Black people in twenty-first-century America stands as a national disgrace, some sixty years after the heyday of the civil rights movement. The average white American in their early thirties holds some $30,000 more in wealth than a Black American of the same age, with that gap growing to more than $250,000 by the late fifties. In December 2022, 3 percent of all Americans in the workforce were unemployed; 5.7 percent of Black Americans were unemployed. The poverty rate of white Americans in 2021 was 9.5 percent, while the poverty rate for Black Americans was 21.7 percent. Some 62.5 percent of white Americans graduate from college within five years of enrollment; 40.5 percent of Black Americans do. In 2019, the average life span for a white American was seventy-nine years, while the average life span for a Black American was seventy-five years. In 2019, 73.3 percent of white Americans owned their homes, while only

42.1 percent of Black Americans did. In 2021, the rate of imprisonment for Black Americans was 1,1240 per 100,000, while the rate for white Americans was 261 per 100,000. In 2020, 6.2 percent of adult Black Americans had been disenfranchised (lost the right to vote) thanks to criminal conviction, compared to only 1.7 percent of the non-Black population. Some of these facts might be subject to qualification or complication, but taken as a whole they are proof that our country has utterly failed to live up to its ideals and left Black people behind.

Those daily inequities were the background against which the drama of 2020 took place. When protesters took to the streets, they were marching for George Floyd, whose murder was seen by billions across the globe and whose death was correctly understood to be a crime of horrific cruelty and historical significance. They were also marching for so many other Black people killed by police. The protests were an expression of feelings of rage, purpose, and shame—shame that a country that prided itself on its freedoms would continue to mete out so much senseless injustice upon the descendants of those brought here in chains. The violence that exploded in some cities may have been unfocused and unhelpful, but I would never call it hard to understand. And in the most basic sense of galvanizing ordinary people to action, those protests were among the rare class of those that were entirely successful. Left protesters are always saying that attention must be paid; in 2020, it was.

The statistical reality of police killings in general—that is to say, how common they are and whether they've gone up or down in recent years—is fiercely debated. But based on the data available to us, the general finding is that about one thousand people are shot and killed by police in the United States per year. According to the *Washington Post*, 1,096 people were killed by police in 2022 specifically—225 of them were Black, while 389 were white (341 were of an unknown race, so each number is no doubt larger than represented by either figure; the remainder are Asian and Hispanic deaths). While more white Americans were shot and killed in total, white Americans made up 59 percent of the American population in 2022 and Black Americans only 14 percent, and so the rate at which Black people were killed was far higher—in fact, Black Americans are twice as likely to be killed by police than white Americans in any given year. There is no way to read that data and fail to see injustice. And the details of so many of the high-profile incidents demonstrate that many of these killings are entirely avoidable. We could also add to this list those killed not by the police but by those acting as vigilantes, such as in the cases of Trayvon Martin and Ahmaud Arbery.

We do, luckily, have a number of policy goals that we can pursue to address this injustice. A good overview can be found in the George Floyd Justice in Policing Act, the sadly failed bill of proposed 2020 and 2021 federal legislation that was the most prominent recent attempt to address policing issues on a national level. Its provisions included

- expanding regulations for federal oversight of local police forces via the Department of Justice's Civil Rights Division;
- providing grants to states to pay for investigations into police misconduct;
- the creation of a federal registry of police misconduct;
- mandating dashboard and body cameras for federal law enforcement officers and creating incentives for their use by state and local police;
- establishing a ban on chokeholds by federal law enforcement and those state and local organizations that receive federal funds;
- banning "no knock" raids by federal law enforcement, that is, police raids in which the police do not announce themselves prior to entering a room or building;

- changing the terms under which federal law enforcement personnel could use deadly force; and
- restricting the application of the qualified immunity doctrine for police officers.

That last bullet point is perhaps the most important. According to the Equal Justice Initiative, qualified immunity is "a court-created rule that limits victims of police violence and misconduct from holding officers accountable when they violate a person's constitutional rights." Qualified immunity applies to civil prosecution of police officers rather than criminal prosecution, but still functions as a major legal shield for police officers and thus an impediment to establishing police accountability. If the police violate your civil rights, you can hope that the police themselves will enforce accountability, which is unlikely for obvious reasons; you can potentially see the prosecution of the police in the criminal justice system, which tends to happen in only the most spectacular abuses, such as with the police officers who murdered George Floyd; or you can sue. The doctrine of qualified immunity makes the latter very, very difficult, and is a big part of the reason that police officers so often act with complete impunity. Any meaningful reform of our criminal justice system must involve the end of qualified immunity.

Discussion of the merits of the George Floyd Justice in Policing Act is largely academic, as the bill died in Congress, though I hope it might be revived. In 2020, Republicans controlled the Senate, and the bill had no chance of passage; in 2021, Democrats held the Senate by the thinnest-possible majority, and the bill died in committee, despite passing the House and public endorsement by President Biden. I found the response to the bill strangely muted, given how much these issues had dominated public consciousness. Of course, failure tends to engender less publicity than success, and Congress is boring. But the inability of our political system to pass a bill that many activists saw as the bare minimum was notable, if for no other reason than to remind us of how hard change would be and that Republican power could not be wished away.

Then again, perhaps the George Floyd Justice in Policing bill failed to attract much attention because it was overshadowed by the demand that became associated with the entire movement for justice that erupted in the wake of George Floyd's death, which became inescapable—"defund the police."

THE STRANGE LIFE OF DEFUND THE POLICE

Defunding the police captured the public attention to a degree that I've really never seen before for a genuinely radical idea. And I believe it hurt the wider cause. I think that, at the exact moment that public support for racial justice was at its zenith, the call to defund the police sapped our attention, sucked the air out of the room, and scuttled the opportunity of more achievable reforms.

The exact meaning of defunding the police was never entirely clear. A meta debate about what exactly was being called for bloomed—and became notorious. For some, its meaning was straightforward: abolition. The end of police departments, of policing and policemen. Again, this was not a new concept. *The End of Policing* by Alex S. Vitale, a sociology professor at the City University of New York, was released just three years before George Floyd's murder and called for an eventual end to policing in its entirety. The book became something like a bible for those who pressed the case for revolutionary change in 2020. The 2003 prison abolition manual *Are Prisons Obsolete?* by civil rights activist legend Angela Davis also was rediscovered, and it too called for abolition in a literal and concrete sense. By calling for defunding the police, some people meant, and still mean, true abolition.

The trouble was that abolishing the police was always, to put it mildly, unachievable. A YouGov poll conducted in late May 2020, when outrage over Floyd's death was inescapable, found that only 16 percent of *Democrats* supported cutting police funding, to say nothing of abolition. Some Democrats representing liberal enclaves, like St. Louis representative Cori Bush, endorsed the idea, but the party ran from it, with Speaker of the House Nancy Pelosi stating flatly, "That is not the position of the Democratic Party." Of course, it's not like they would have been successful if it were. Even setting aside what would have been unprecedentedly visceral opposition from centrists and conservatives, policing in the United States is largely a state and local affair, and efforts to end it would have required waging a war on an endless number of local fronts. This reality lent the whole affair a strange atmosphere of unreality; everyone knew that we weren't going to defund the police, and yet it had become such a dominant bit of lefty fashion that just as many continued robotically making the demand anyway. As I've said, it was a strange time.

The concept of the end of policing and prisons was not new in 2020. There have been leftists advocating for police and prison abolition for as long as I've been politically conscious. Activists demanding the abolition of police had a large corpus of theoretical writing to draw from. But there was usually a key difference between the older school of police and prison abolition and the demands of the most impassioned days of 2020: the former almost always imagined that a world without formal policing would emerge only after other society-altering changes had taken place. Typically, this was defined as the fall of capitalism and the establishment of some sort of socialist system, a system without poverty and deprivation. In other words, the radicals I knew might imagine the end of the police, but they imagined that end would come after the revolution. To debate the concept in 2020 was to skip a lot of steps. This was a general issue in the first year after Floyd's murder, a sense that people wanted to dodge the hard work that would have been necessary before society-altering changes could take place.

In part because of the extremely low odds of success for a police abolition movement, many who supported defunding the police insisted that the intent had never been to abolish the police at all. In this telling, "defund the police" means reducing the budgets of police departments, drawing down their resources, and redirecting some of those funds to other uses, such as social work and emergency medical services. Sometimes activists describe this as "unbundling" the police departments, identifying purposes other than the use of socially sanctioned force to establish order and removing those purposes from the purview of the police. I find little to object to in these proposals, but it's worth saying that they represent a profound mismatch between the revolutionary zeal of the people who called to defund the police and the actual policy. It also represents a good example of "sanewashing," an internet term that refers to the process through which radical ideas are gradually watered down to be more appealing to the wider public. You will easily imagine how this played out in 2020—the call to defund the police was inescapable on left-leaning social media; decent people who were outraged about Floyd's murder wanted to support the cause, but the concept of police abolition was too radical for them to express. So they did some sanewashing and came up with a more palatable version.

At times, supporters of the more watered-down version of defunding the police would insist that no one would ever call for total abolition. It was therefore somewhat useful when, in June, the *New York Times* published the aforementioned opinion piece, "Yes, We Mean Literally Abolish the Police." That piece, written with considerable brio, does not include anything like a plan.

Many liberals and lefties still support defunding the police in the abstract, but there's little sense of a specific vehicle for how that would be accomplished. A handful of municipalities meaningfully redistributed resources away from police in 2020, but no national movement followed. It's impossible to say what might have happened in a world where defund the police did not become the most-expressed demand associated with the George Floyd moment. I would certainly have been thrilled if "end qualified immunity" had gained similar prominence. Supporters of defunding the police, of course, would point out that the effort to end qualified immunity has not seen much more tangible success than the movement to defund the police, and they would have a point. As is so often the case, the most essential question is one of the hardest to answer—what are the boundaries of the possible in both the short or long term?

Perhaps someday we will have the wisdom and equanimity toward the guilty to truly abolish prisons, and perhaps someday we'll have eliminated poverty and need to such a degree that we can abolish policing. Until then, defunding the police strikes me the same way it did during that tense summer: as a distraction from doing something meaningful to mitigate injustice.

THE BLACK PROFESSIONAL-MANAGERIAL CLASS SPEAKS

The deeper question confronting America's anti-racism movement is the degree to which police violence is the right frame for dealing with racial inequality writ large. Certainly, the reaction to George Floyd's murder demonstrates the power of the image of yet another Black victim of police brutality. I only wish more of the rage of 2020—a righteous rage, a justifiable rage—had been pressed into the service of reducing the daily iniquities and injustices. It's here that the distance between the Black professional class and the average Black American was so consequential: the spectacular horrors of police murder were always more apt to attract national attention than the daily economic depravations that Black members of the chattering class are less likely to experience.

Black Lives Matter has a dual nature: it was born of the rage and horror that attends unjustified police killing of Black people but weaves them into the broader reality of American racism. This is not only a reasonable way to build that movement but also the *only* way to build it. The broad and diffuse nature of racial inequality can best be confronted by showing people the expression of that inequality through individual acts of injustice, and extrajudicial killings by agents of the state are a particularly horrific example. But this has also proven to be part of the difficulty the movement has faced in effecting change; the focus on the specific problem of police killings orients the movement toward a very specific problem rather than toward the many more general problems Black Americans face. And it's fair to ask about where we would best put our political resources. This question stems from the fact that the unjustified killing of Black people by the police is horrific, a clear expression of racism, a vestige of the communal tendency to see Black Americans as dangerous, all too common, and, by any measure, rare.

"Too common" and "rare" may feel difficult to parse, but both are true. We should take care to balance several different thoughts at once. The first is to say that any number of innocent people killed by the police is too many. I am opposed to the death penalty even when it involves years of lengthy trials and appeals; I'm certainly opposed to a police officer handing out such a sentence on their own in a snap decision. And being killed by the state's security forces is especially heinous, as extrajudicial murder by those tasked with maintaining order for society undermines communal faith in the entire system. At the same time, we should also be accurate and realistic about the size of the problem, and not exaggerate the threat of police murder among Black people or anyone else. The threat of being killed by the police is real and unusually disturbing, but that risk, for anyone, is extraordinarily low in basic quantitative terms. These thoughts are not difficult to balance.

Then there's the (incorrect) insistence that any given interaction between a Black person and the police presents a great risk of the death of that Black person, which has real stakes in our debates. We can see this clearly in the story of the "Central Park Karen." On Memorial Day 2020, the same day as George Floyd's murder, a white woman walking her dog in Central Park got into an altercation with a Black birdwatcher. As their confrontation escalated, she threatened to call the police and eventually did, falsely claiming that he had threatened her. A video of their encounter went mega viral, and she proceeded to face immense consequences: receiving many death threats, losing her job, having her dog temporarily taken from her, feeling compelled to flee the country, and being arrested on charges of filing a false police report. Those charges were eventually dropped, after she took a racial sensitivity course, thanks in part to the birdwatcher's refusal to participate in her prosecution. But she initially faced a year in prison, and many of the online commentariat expressed anger over the dismissal of the charges.

Whether the Central Park Karen deserves any sympathy is not my interest here. I am however interested in the underlying logic behind the anger toward her. What was said again and again was that she was guilty of putting a Black man's life in mortal danger by calling the police. This attitude became generally prevalent in 2020, the idea that involving the police in any given incident risks the lives of Black people, and posturing white liberals bragged online that they would never call the police for any reason. (This was even enforced purely in the abstract, as when the *New York Times* published an op-ed by Arkansas senator Tom Cotton calling on the military to confront looters; the paper's staff revolted, based on the rather dubious claim that the piece endangered the lives of Black *NYT* employees.) Calling the police is always an extreme action and should not be undertaken lightly, and there are types of racial bias that the police engage in beyond physical violence. But it's worth pointing out that the idea that any specific encounter between Black people and the police is likely to result in deadly violence cannot withstand scrutiny. There were no doubt millions of interactions between the police and Black citizens in 2022, and 225 Black people were killed by police officers. Of course this number is far too high. Of course this situation demands immediate redress. But there are some forty-seven million Black Americans, and so the odds of any specific interaction between police and Black people ending in a police killing are incredibly low. And this matters not because of a desire to exonerate any given white person from calling the police on a Black person inappropriately, but because we do Black Americans no favors by cultivating an unrealistic level of fear about police killing.

If you're afraid that taking a dispassionate view of the rate of police killings of Black people will dull our sense of the continuing mass racial injustice that permeates the United States, we could always pay attention instead to all the other ways that police mistreat and oppress Black people. We're not going to run out of reasons to indict American policing.

That the average Black American faces little statistical risk of being killed by the police is reflected in Black attitudes toward policing in the United States. Because despite the rhetoric that emanates from Black Lives Matter and its many champions in the media, polling has shown again and again that Black respondents do not want significantly reduced police presence in their communities; in fact, they frequently call for more. This is a very durable finding in polling. Pew Research Center, for example, found that in June 2020, at the height of the George Floyd protest moment, 55 percent of Black respondents wanted police spending in their area to stay the same or to grow; by September 2021, that number had grown to 76 percent. Similarly, a Gallup poll from August 2020 found that 81 percent of Black respondents wanted the police presence in their area to stay constant or grow. An October 2022 poll of Black voters from TheGrio and the Kaiser Family Foundation found that only 17 percent supported decreasing funding for the police. There are many more such findings.

What we have here is a microcosm of a much broader reality in contemporary liberal politics: the tastemakers who define our political moment—who are the very ones with the ability to participate in the national political conversation—are out of step with everyday citizens from the constituencies they ostensibly speak for. The concept of defunding the police played out loudly in our discourse, but this phenomenon was driven by elites whose day-to-day lives are far removed from ordinary people, and especially ordinary Black Americans. This was true of not only the predominately white political class that sets the national conversation but also the Black writers, academics, and activists who helped to define what BLM is and means. Correspondingly, these activists had different perspectives on policing and on how to reform it.

How to reform policing. Not *whether* to reform it. The resistance to reducing police funding or presence should not in any way suggest that Black Americans were or are satisfied with the state of community policing. A June 2022 poll from the Gallup Center on Black Voices found that 50 percent of respondents overall and 72 percent of Black respondents wanted major changes to American policing. This too is a common outcome in polling. There is no contradiction between these two findings: it appears significant majorities of Black Americans want not less policing but better policing. That is an internally consistent point of view, even if it's out of step with elite liberal opinion. For all the common corruption and abuse that it's subject to, policing represents a public service.

The described dynamics aren't a matter of a divide just between Black activists and Black citizens but also between white liberals and the rest of the Democratic Party. As a piece from the Survey Center on American Life pointed out, "on a number of racial issues, white liberals do not align with Democratic-leaning Black and Hispanic voters. . . . One reason that cutting police budgets may not resonate with Black and Hispanic Americans is that these groups are much more concerned about crime." The piece makes clear that for decades Black respondents have consistently been more likely to identify crime as a major issue or top priority than white liberals. This reality cuts directly against the conventional wisdom about race in the United States in recent years, but it makes perfect sense if you actually think about it. People who are more likely to be the victims of violent crime are more likely to want police presence in their community to attempt to prevent it; people who have less financial ability to replace stolen property are more likely to be concerned about property crime.

Here's another forbidden fact: Research indicates that more policing does reduce crime. A 2020 paper from the National Bureau of Economic Research, for example, found that more cops on the beat reduced homicides, and particularly so in the Black community. There's a long history of similar findings. In and of itself, this observation can't serve as a response to critiques of racism in American policing and does not in any sense reduce the need for broad and deep reform. But it does suggest that police abolition and incremental efforts to reduce policing could easily result in more hardship for the very community that we're ostensibly fighting for. Because if we take any honest appraisal of the biggest challenges facing the Black community, we must list crime near the top. If I haven't already lost the typical liberal reader in this chapter, I will surely lose them here, as I feel compelled to discuss violence against the Black community that does not involve the police, including, I'm afraid, "Black-on-Black crime."

Such discussion has long had a bad reputation within the left-of-center and engaging in it has become right-coded. To consider violence within the Black community, rather than only that inflicted upon the Black community by the police, has become verboten in much of the progressive community. The reason for this avoidance is not hard to define, and, in fact, this tendency is quite understandable: responding to discussion of police violence by reflexively discussing Black-on-Black crime is a common conservative trope. Talking about gang violence or similar in the face of calls for justice over police violence against Black people is the worst kind of dodge; it affects concern for Black people while simultaneously distracting from one of their chief concerns. It should go without saying, but the prevalence of nonpolice assault and murder against Black people cannot stand as an excuse for police assault and murder of Black people, and to pit one against the other is to misunderstand both problems.

Yet I feel that the social prohibition against ever discussing violence and crime committed against Black people that does not emanate from the police is misguided. Yes, such talk can be a distraction and a dodge. But surely there is time enough to have a full and critical accounting of police violence against Black people while also paying attention to the Black community's greater exposure to crime and violence in general. And, indeed, there is a robust conversation about crime in the Black community taking place within that community. As I've mentioned, polling of Black Americans consistently finds that they list crime as a higher priority or more important issue than the overall average. Municipal elections in majority-Black cities often feature candidates wrestling to be perceived as the toughest on crime. There are also hundreds of organizations across the United States, many or most of them Black-led, that are dedicated to reducing the burden of violence on the Black community. Consider, for example, the Community Justice Action Fund, whose website reads "Community Justice works to end gun violence in Black and Brown communities, by empowering those closest to the pain to build political power, change the narrative and advocate for policy change."

The statistics about violence and crime committed against Black Americans are arresting. According to the FBI, Black Americans are annually about 2.5 times more likely to be the victim of violent crime than the national average. FBI data also shows that Black Americans are 2.5 times more likely to be murdered than the national average. In 2022, the *Washington Post* summarized this reality, and reflected on a pandemic-era surge in murders, saying:

> In 2020 those identifying or identified as Black or African American made up 13.5 percent of the U.S. population, according to CDC estimates. . . . They also made up 55.6 percent of the homicide victims, and 65.6 percent of the increase in homicides relative to 2019. To put it another way, the homicide rate for Black Americans rose from 22.9 per 100,000 in 2019 to 30.7 in 2020. For all other Americans, the rate went from 3.2 to 3.8.

What makes this conversation particularly touchy is that most of these crimes against Black Americans are committed by Black Americans. Yet this potentially fraught point must be immediately put into context: People of *all* races are disproportionately likely to be killed by people of their own race. In 2018, for example, 81 percent of white victims were killed by white offenders, while 89 percent of Black victims were killed by Black offenders, again according to the FBI. This is a vestige of a simple (if somewhat gloomy) reality of American life: most people primarily associate with other members of their own race, spend time with members of their own race. With more interactions, there's more opportunity for violence. The trouble is therefore not that Black Americans are unusually likely to target each other but rather that the basal rates of violent crimes generally—and homicide specifically—are so much higher than for other racial groups.

Many books have been written about the reasons for the higher rates of crime committed by and against Black Americans. I won't try to make a half-assed gloss on them, other than to suggest that these conditions are no doubt the product of a vast number of disparate variables. Beyond that, I will leave the question to the sociologists. What I can tell you is that, especially in the post–George Floyd era of American race relations, the progressive left in the contemporary United States seems almost entirely unwilling to even broach the subject. I feel strongly that there must be a way—there must be a way—to take police violence against Black people immensely seriously and to fight for major police reform while acknowledging that crimes and violence committed against Black people by those other than police are far more common.

The trouble, again, is elite control over the discourse. To begin with, there's the influence of those white liberals on the conversation. It's a bare fact about American political life that most of our racial discourse is dictated by white people. This is a simple matter of majorities: most Americans are white, and an even higher percentage of those with college degrees or who work in media and academia or are involved in the political process—those who can most influence the political discussion—are white. And a great deal of the debates that attended the tumult of 2020 and the years surrounding it had the quality of white people talking to each other. No doubt most white people engaged in these debates were motivated by a sincere desire to do the right thing. But the interests of white people can be so inescapable in American intellectual life that they can generate a kind of gravity from which nothing escapes. And there were obvious social and professional advantages for many white people in publicly supporting the calls for racial justice; being seen as a committed ally was a cheap way to engage in self-aggrandizement while appearing to be selfless. But the kind of college-educated white people who filled so much of the air in these conversations can necessarily know little about the lived experience of the average Black American.

A white liberal in 2020 might have fixated relentlessly on defunding the police, for example, because there was social benefit in appearing to be radical and because they themselves had little to gain from focusing on far more likely and practical reforms. After all, they weren't the ones facing such greater risk of being murdered, nor were they the ones likely to benefit from modest but meaningful police reforms. Meanwhile, the average Black Americans who actually stood to gain from such reform to our system had little ability to participate in the national conversation.

The philosopher Liam Kofi Bright has written about this dynamic. In 2022, he published a paper titled "White Psychodrama," which argues that a lot of what passes for racial discourse in contemporary times amounts to, indeed, white psychodrama. As Bright points out, a great deal of our "conversation about race" is filtered through the guilt and fear of white people—the guilt of being part of the dominant class in a deeply unequal society and the fear of being labeled a racist. There are different ways that white liberals respond to those guilts and fears, and different levels of sophistication in managing the psychodrama. But the inter-white liberal conflict is fundamentally "a conflict over how to psychologically manage the results of living in a materially deeply unequal society, not a conflict about how or whether to reduce that material inequality." When the risk of being publicly indicted for racial insensitivity grew in response to police abuses, so too did the perceived social stakes for white people—which meant that, perversely, when the need for a racial reckoning was most clear, so were the incentives for white people to make the conversation about racial justice all about them.

It's easy to indict white liberals. (They spend a lot of time indicting themselves.) The more controversial point, and more essential, is this: as is always the case with a movement and those it speaks for, the activists who powered Black Lives Matter were not representative of Black Americans writ large. As with activists from all groups, BLM activists are unalike the people they speak for in myriad ways. I've already discussed consistent polling that shows that Black Americans are deeply opposed to the basic notion of defunding the police. It's worth saying that Black Democrats, which many people identify as the heart of the party, tend to self-identify as moderates, not liberals—far more so than white Democrats. As the Pew Research Center noted in 2020, "In 2019, about four in ten Black Democratic voters called themselves moderate, while smaller shares described their views as liberal (29 percent) or conservative (25 percent). By contrast, 37 percent of Hispanic and 55 percent of white Democratic voters identified as liberal." Indeed, thanks to their centrist tendencies and higher religiosity than the rest of the Democratic coalition, Black Democrats have long acted as a moderating force on the party as a whole.

Black Lives Matter activists, it's fair to say, did not represent this Black majority. The movement has always been large and amorphous, and in 2020, many millions of people who had never before participated in the then-six-year-old movement were suddenly radicalized. Famously, there is no one specific official organization that speaks for BLM, though several, such as the Movement for Black Lives, are frequently cited as leaders. There is therefore no possibility of speaking about the makeup of the movement with quantitative rigor. But I feel quite confident in saying that the typical activist who marched and spoke and lobbied on behalf of Black Lives Matter was dramatically better educated than the average American; he or she spoke a different language, held different values, came from different philosophical assumptions. The most prominent Black voices in 2020 were not like the median Black American, who is in early middle age, has some college but no degree, resides in the lower middle class, and votes as a moderate Democrat. BLM activists were, instead, largely an army of graduate students and professors, journalists and pundits, writers and actors, and, of course, professional organizers from nonprofits. They were a self-selected group of people who had been motivated by their conscience.

They have been, in other words, members of the Black professional-managerial class, or PMC—the late socialist critics John and Barbara Ehrenreich's term for those whose position involves higher levels of education than the norm, occupations that are heavily involved in communicative or administrative practice, and whose technocratic skills give them advantages not just in the professional domain but in spreading their political priorities or values. The average BLM organizer certainly enjoyed an educational advantage over the Black median, and thus almost certainly an advantage in income. But more than anything, they were more media savvy, in better position to use the vocabulary of elite America, and both more eager and able to define what success meant for Black Lives Matter. We might refer to BLM therefore as BPMCLM—Black Professional-Managerial Class Lives Matter.

It's difficult to speak frankly about the existence of the Black professional-managerial class because that existence cuts against the thoughtless-but-common assuming away of Black success. Since emancipation, there has always been a Black upper class, just as there is with any group of people. The Black upper class has been smaller and held less average wealth than the upper-class norm, thanks to racial inequality, but it does exist. The erasure of that class comes from two directions at once: racism suggests that Black people are all poor, while anti-racism tends to push people to avoid talking about the Black middle and upper classes for fear of encouraging complacency about racial justice. (Margo Jefferson's memoir *Negroland* made great hay out of the invisibility of the Black professional class.)

There's another reason for the tendency to minimize the Black PMC in our discourse: the allergy to acknowledging progress in racial issues. Our media discussion on race and racism, which is largely led by left-leaning people, tends to avoid acknowledging when things are getting better regarding race and racism. There just isn't much incentive to declaring that things have improved; doing so exposes you to accusations that you are overlooking the large enduring racial inequality that exists. But some things have gotten better. In 1940, Black high school students graduated at 27 percent of the national average, while in 2020, the gap was less than 3 percent; in 1940, Black college graduates were 26 percent as likely to have a bachelor's degree; in 2019, they were 73 percent as likely. In a country where racial progress has been so hard to come by, increasing rates of education of Black students has been a clear area of growth. Correspondingly, in our industries that are devoted to intellectual and communicative production—such as media, academia, and nonprofits—there has been real progress, particularly since the birth of Black Lives Matter in 2014. For one example, from 2018 to 2019 (prior to recent widespread post-2020 diversification efforts), Black leads in broadcast shows increased from 8.3 percent to 11.6 percent and in cable shows from 12.9 percent to 14.1 percent. Since the George Floyd protests, media companies, universities, and charitable foundations have made major efforts to hire more Black employees. There are far more Black voices in the national conversation now than there were even a decade ago—which means that there is more opportunity for a divide between the Black chattering class and the Black norm.

That BLM activists are not identical to the Black public is neither surprising nor nefarious; activists are not meant to serve as representatives of median public opinion but as agents of change. Political movements have always been driven by a vanguard. (When I first started protesting the invasion of Afghanistan, to pick one example of many, the war was wildly popular.) Black activists must similarly pursue the dictates of their heart. The trouble is not that Black Lives Matter activists and supporters don't hew exactly to existing Black opinion but that the social distance between them and the median Black American risks focusing our attention on issues important to the activist class rather than to Black people

66

writ large. And what has defined so much of contemporary race politics has been an obsessive focus on using the correct language and using the right symbols.

Correspondingly, the institutions most affected have been those most dedicated to the linguistic and the symbolic—academia, entertainment, news media, the offices in government that make decisions about communication. One of the most obvious changes that arose was the formation of new language codes—unofficial and implied, particularly on social media, but also official guides to appropriate terminology at universities, in newspapers and magazines, in movies and shows. For example, in 2020 attendees of the Conference on College Composition and Communication, the largest professional gathering of educators and administrators who work in college writing, developed a list of demands for how language should evolve in the classroom in light of Black Lives Matter, including "We demand that teachers stop using academic language and standard English as the accepted communicative norm, which reflects white mainstream English!" and "We demand Black linguistic consciousness!" (The list was titled "This Ain't Another Statement! This is a DEMAND for Black Linguistic Justice!" From the perspective of a few years later, it certainly appears to have been just another statement.)

We should take care not to underestimate the achievement of the Black Lives Matter protest movement itself; whatever their distance from the opinion of the average Black voter, and however we might question what has happened since, the Black-led protest movement really did shake the entire world, for a time. I don't want to gloss over what they accomplished. In the philosopher's Olúfẹ́mi O. Táíwò's *Elite Capture*, which is all about the tendency of elites to take over the social justice movement, he took care to praise "this global solidarity [which] undoubtedly owes itself to the steadfast international organizing work of Black Lives Matter chapters." We should take care to acknowledge that accomplishment as well. But we should also be clear-eyed that some of the most obvious outcomes of all of this protesting were language games and policing of the symbolic in a few elite industries.

ASKING FOR MORE

The content of these fundamentally symbolic codes of conduct can be debated. What's not debatable is that they exist at a remove from the brick-and-mortar realities that are influenced by racism—unequal policing, lack of economic opportunity, inability to access health care, housing insecurity. Consider, for example, the voicing of Black animated characters by voice actors who are not Black. When the culture was raging with passion for racial justice, some Black characters in animated shows that had previously been played by actors of other races were recast. Personally, I'm not at all moved by the idea that every actor should play only characters with whom they share every personal attribute. (That's why it's called acting.) But setting my personal disagreement with the wisdom of this attitude aside . . . could this really be a response to watching an innocent man be strangled to death in the street? How did our attention wander so far from the basic human needs that truly propel the cry for change?

When announcing that she was giving up a role on the show *Big Mouth*, the actor Jenny Slate said, "At the start of the show, I reasoned with myself that it was permissible for me to play Missy because her mom is Jewish and white—as am I. But Missy is also Black, and Black characters on an animated show should be played by Black people."

My God. What sacrifice.

George Floyd was killed in the street, and an actor gave up a voice-over gig.

George Floyd was killed in the street, and investment banks adopted new corporate sensitivity policies. George Floyd was killed in the street, and defense contractors updated their employee handbooks. George Floyd was killed in the street, and universities made their language codes for faculty even more stringent.

George Floyd was killed in the street, and the term "BIPOC"— that's Black and Indigenous people of color, to better highlight the most oppressed—replaced "people of color," itself a replacement of older terms. This is the way left politics works now: we respond to tangible horror by clinging tighter and tighter to the intangible. Perhaps the effort to make interpersonal relations between white and Black people more respectful for the latter sometimes works. Again, this fixation on the linguistic makes some sense for those whose professions are fundamentally linguistic in nature. But it's profoundly hard to see how those interpersonal politics could make Black people richer, safer, or more free.

In a 2014 paper for the Public Autonomy Project, the philosopher Stephen D'Arcy reflected on the tendency of new activist vocabularies to foreground the personal over the systemic, to the detriment of achieving structural change. Radical politics, in other words, has changed from being a matter of pursuing systemic progress and instead become a matter of moral hygiene, of saying rather than of doing. While D'Arcy recognizes the need for respect and justice in interpersonal interactions, he also wrote that "the Left needs a vocabulary, and a self-understanding, that highlights and foregrounds the importance of constructing and expanding anti-systemic movements that aim to defeat systems of oppressive and exploitative power." That is, we need to put systems before interpersonal niceties. Speaking of the radical left of an earlier age, he said, "It is hard not to think that the older vocabulary better expresses this insight." This is precisely what I am attempting to do here, to demonstrate that the now old-fashioned focus on power and structural injustice was a better frame for achieving racial progress. Reflecting in 1966 on the difficulty the civil rights movement faced after its victories with the Civil Rights

Act and Voting Rights Act, Martin Luther King Jr. wrote that "Negroes have benefited from a limited change that was emotionally satisfying but materially deficient."

This is not a popular perspective. The trouble with denouncing the preeminence of the linguistic and the symbolic is that people whose professions are fundamentally linguistic and symbolic (artists, writers, journalists, academics) are empowered in this scenario. That it damages our ability to make real change typically goes unsaid. And those who benefit most are, frequently, people of color themselves, who insist on the dominance of the symbolic as a matter of self-preservation. As Bright wrote in his paper on white psychodrama, "How then have the PoC intelligentsia—people of colour sufficiently engaged in politics to be tapped into the white culture war and the historical narrative underpinning it—responded to the opportunities and challenges presented thereby? . . . By cashing in."

I have little doubt that those who take part in the racial politics of symbolism and language believe they're doing the best for the movement. It's no wonder they're trapped in symbols; symbols are all they know. In more tangible and sadder terms, Black Lives Matter has not been free from more naked types of self-interest. As in any area of human affairs, there is the question of simple corruption. A *lot* of money was raised for Black Lives Matter–related causes in 2020 and the years since. According to the *Washington Post*, the top fifty American corporations raised $50 billion for BLM-related purposes between George Floyd's death and August 2021, though much of this money was not immediately accessible for charitable work. Individual donors and independent philanthropic organizations no doubt raised billions more; an *Economist* article suggested that some $10.6 billion had been raised by October 2020.

Whatever the exact figures, the amount of money donated in the name of Black Lives Matter in the past several years must rival that donated after the 9/11 attacks; it's an immense amount of money. The trouble is that it's very hard to know where all that money went, as there's no overarching agency that can perform an audit. But what we know is not encouraging. A January 2022 investigation by *New York* magazine found rife mismanagement and a lack of clear accounting in BLM-associated groups; the same reporter later discovered that the Black Lives Matter Global Network Foundation, an organization that includes several people who are known as early leaders of BLM, had secretly purchased a six-million-dollar home for its founders. This is, to put it mildly, a little disappointing.

Show me a political movement, and I'll show you those who find a way to profit off it; profiteering is endemic to political striving. There's no need to hang such an accusation on Black Lives Matter uniquely. Still, I have to point out that the discussion of the alleged misuse of funds has been muted, no doubt because many don't want to risk appearing to criticize the movement. But the only way to make a movement work is to have a full accounting of its resources and how they're spent.

There's another kind of profiteering that arose from the 2020 moment, a special kind of race hustler who looked at the horror and rage and saw a market opportunity. Some lucky people made a lot of money selling books, for example; the (conspicuously white) author Robin DiAngelo's book *White Fragility*, while written before Floyd's death, became a towering bestseller in 2020, as untold hundreds of thousands of white people looked to be psychically punished for their privilege. *White Fragility* is something like a textbook for treating racial inequality as a matter of interpersonal niceties rather than as a flesh-and-blood reality that is embedded in the structures of American life. Not to be undone, the "racial educators" Saira Rao and Regina Jackson began an endeavor called Race2Dinner in which white women paid upward of $5,000 to sit through a dinner party during which they were ritualistically flogged for failing to interrogate their white privilege. (The doctrine of racism as a matter of manners is obsessed with white people interrogating their privilege, wrestling with their privilege, reckoning with their privilege, and doing other vague things with their privilege.) In a 2021 story about Race2Dinner in *New York* magazine, the company's token white-woman employee Lisa Bond was quoted as saying, "This idea that we, as white people, need to go out and make these big external actions—that's just white supremacy. . . . This internal work is the hard work; it's the work that never ends."

This is something like my worst nightmare: a white woman insisting that fighting racism is a predominately internal affair, that fighting Black poverty or cleaning Black environments of lead or preventing crime against Black victims is all subordinate to white people feeling guilty. This is what 2020 amounted to for far too many white people, an endorsement of their psychodrama. All of that righteous anger, all of those days of rage in the streets, led to this: a white person insisting, with impeccable confidence, that to want to end the material oppression of Black people was itself a vestige of white supremacy. And while plenty of people made fun of that quote and the article in which it appeared, to this day there has been no accounting for—no reckoning with—how we fell so far, so fast.

When Barack Obama was elected in 2008, many left-leaning people rushed to point out that his election did not mean that racism was over. Which, of course, it wasn't. In particular, many commentators admonished others that we should not be seduced into thinking that we were living in a "post-racial America." Which, of course, we aren't. This tendency had that classic status where the denunciations were more prevalent than that which was being denounced; in the years since Obama's election, I have seen vastly more people arguing that we don't live in a post-racial America than arguing that we do. Still, the point was wise. We don't live in a post-racial America, and we won't until we achieve total equality between the races.

But something strange happened over time. The argument changed from being that we *did not yet* live in a post-racial America—and shouldn't be fooled into thinking we did—to an argument that the very desire to live in a post-racial America was wicked. This is a slide that pops up constantly in the diversity, equity, and inclusion trainings that so many people sleepwalk through at work, that desiring a post-racial America is racist. (Ostensibly, these trainings are led out of an organic desire to reduce racism in the workplace; as a practical matter, holding such workshops can be used by employers as evidence that they care about reducing racism in the workplace, in the event of a discrimination lawsuit.) Savvy people now know better than to yearn for a post-racial America, one where people aren't prejudged according to their racial categories. If the past several years of American racial politics have taught us anything, it's that the only racial progress that really matters is forcing all of us to think and talk about race, more and more and more often. We can't make Black people safe and free. But we can force people to feel bad about it.

Well—I don't agree. I do think that the point of all of this is, someday in the far future, to achieve a post-racial society. Only after all the hard work, of course. But the fixation on racism (excuse me, white supremacy) as the sole motivating force of all human affairs does not seem like progress. I just don't think making every last permutation of American politics a part of our racial dialogue is actually helping us to tear down racial inequality. And frankly, I don't think most regular people, of any race, want our obsession with race to deepen even further. I find it remarkable that the following statement might likely be controversial: while race permeates American politics, and while any political topic you can think of will intersect with issues of race, race is not the sole orienting principle of human life. Race is a big thing, but it is not everything. Race is an essential lens for understanding the world, but it is not the only lens.

These statements feel anodyne to me, quotidian, and yet experience teaches me that they're considered fighting words. I was in grad school from 2009 to 2015, during which time I got an MA and PhD. And even within that brief period, the pressure to incorporate racial issues into all our academic work grew significantly. By the mid-2010s, almost every aspiring academic I knew was laboring to emphasize the racial elements of their work, and everyone scrambled to find ways to represent themselves as a "diverse" candidate for various laurels and job searches. The result, in my opinion, was a lot of scholarly work with racial elements awkwardly bolted on to them, engaging in liberal academic boilerplate, adding little in the way of sense or meaning. But the graduate students doing this clumsy stitching were only responding to the incentives of the institutions around them, where conferences, publications, and employers demanded ever-more intense focus on race, where only work about "the marginalized" and the injustice they face was treated as being worthy of attention. And all of these dynamics have only deepened since 2020.

The fundamental question is: Do Black people want to think in terms of racial politics all the time? Both the history and continuing reality of American racism forces them to think in racial terms more often than members of any other race. But it seems unlikely to me that the average Black person wants to be seen as a vessel for all of America's long and dark racial history all the time. I've often reflected on the fact that, as a white person, I enjoy the opportunity to not feel racialized whenever I'm not explicitly considering race. When I walk around in the city, going about my day, I don't think of myself as a white American; I'm simply me. And this is an attitude that's not afforded to people of other races, who often feel that they are racialized at all times. Black writers like W. E. B. Du Bois and Ralph Ellison described that reality decades ago. At times I can't help but wonder if the absolutely monomaniacal liberal fixation on race ultimately deepens this dynamic and so hurts people of color. It makes it that much harder for them to escape, and all of us sometimes need an escape.

The "racial turn" in politics has been good to the degree that it has resulted in racial progress. The question is . . . has it resulted in racial progress? Evidence for such progress is thin on the ground. The bad reasoning at play here is that more talking about race means more progress for people of color, particularly Black people. But if the internet era has proven anything, it's that a lot of talking does not lead us closer to justice. The dynamics of online life mean that the past few years have seen far more public discussion of race and racism than occurred in the heyday of the civil rights movement. I do not need to tell you which period saw greater material progress toward racial equality.

The urge to put the symbolic before the material, to police language rather than to convince the skeptical, to insist that racism is a problem of moral hygiene rather than a flesh-and-blood reality that lies entirely outside the human mind—all of this is a matter of convenience. A matter of convenience because progress has been so hard to come by for so long. If today's anti-racist warriors are guilty of wandering further and further away from basic issues of material security and comfort for Black people, and deeper and deeper into the rabbit hole of language policing and linguistic politics, the most likely reason is because we seem to have lost our ability to make real change. We've turned inward because we have given up.

What I want is Black people in stable homes and Black children in clean and well-resourced schools and Black mothers surviving childbirth and Black men employed and Black families in environments free from contaminants and the Black race freed from fear of unequal and violent policing. Today, each of those essential human goods is rarer and harder to secure for Black Americans than for white; anyone who does not comprehend this reality, and is not willing to do what it takes to fix it, should not be taken seriously. Racism and racial inequality are real, they hang a heavy burden over all people of color, and in both statistical terms and through a basic apprehension of the world around us, no group suffers more from these problems than Black people.

But the most important three words in the preceding paragraph are "what it takes." This is the problem that truly arrests the racial justice movement today: not the *what*, or the *why*, but the *how*. And it's there, I fear, that we have taken several steps backward, in precisely the years in which many liberals have been congratulating themselves for their dedication to justice. There is one quote that defines my understanding of racism and how to fight it better than any other, and it comes from the great activist Stokely Carmichael, later known as Kwame Ture, who has been reported to have said in speeches, "If a white man wants to lynch me, that's his problem. If he's got the power to lynch me, that's my problem. Racism is not a question of attitude; it's a question of power."

He who understands this understands why the twenty-first-century anti-racism movement has failed.

We have gone from marches on Washington to demand jobs and demonstrations to support striking Black garbage workers to millions of decent white liberals clutching "anti-racist" books on the subway, reading about why they're wicked and should feel bad, ensuring that their next interaction with a Black coworker will be strained and awkward, and lining the pockets of white editors, white publishers, sometimes white authors in doing so. And a cottage industry of educators and ideologues have sprung up to say that those feelings themselves—the *feeling* of white guilt, the feeling of white shame—that those feelings are themselves the stuff of anti-racism, that engendering them is victory in and of itself. Meanwhile, in cold apartments lined with lead paint, hungry Black children hide from the violence that grips their neighborhoods. This is the reality of racial justice in twenty-first-century America.

There is another way, one that is relentlessly material and that keeps Carmichael's wisdom in mind at all times. Its victories are harder to achieve than the feelings-based approach. But they are also deeper and more durable.

I don't want white women to clutch their purses a little tighter when a Black man gets on the subway. I don't want white people to maintain internal, emotional prejudice against Black people. But when I look at the mess that the modern anti-racist movement has made of its own mission, and I see the deprivation that so many Black people live with as I make my way around Brooklyn, I think of white people quietly harboring impure racial feelings and all I can think is . . . who cares?

3

MY PROTEST, YOUR RIOT

"We've got to *do something.*" It's a cry I've heard at organizing meetings all my life and seen thrown around on social media regularly. Sometimes we've even got to "*really* do something." What that "something" actually might be is usually not very well defined but when it is clear, it's some type of direct action, often a violent action. There are many commonplaces to life on the radical-left spaces; few are more common, or sadder, than the demand for political violence.

The psychology of such demands is not hard to understand. To be an American radical is to grow used to failure. The two major parties are, at best, a far-right party and a center-left party. My inclination is to describe the Democrats as a center-right party, at least for most of the past fifty years. The number of members of Congress who can legitimately be called leftist, at present, can be counted on two hands. The labor movement that was for generations the engine of progressive social change is moribund, the victim of a hundred years of vicious conservative attacks and the accumulation of unfavorable state laws. Left-wing causes suffer without the infrastructure necessary to harness the motivation for change, while (as we will see) the nonprofits that we do control tend to blunt political energy rather than focus it. There is no national working-class party to put a leftist agenda on the table. We lack the numbers to demand real change and the organizations that could harness those numbers to achieve it.

Meanwhile, our moral demands are immense—by necessity, given the immorality of our system. Some lucky centrists out there could have the country they desire with a few minor tweaks, but the leftists need systemic change. The left calls for a world without poverty; without racism; without sexism; without rule by an autocratic elite; without domination by the wealthy; without environmental devastation; without vast socioeconomic inequality; without hunger or lack of shelter for the poor; without war. These are, obviously, extravagant demands, but this is one of the rare cases where extravagance is no luxury. These demands are founded in basic moral need, and I will never apologize for arguing that we can and must achieve all of them, not in a hundred years or a thousand but now. But the universe is indifferent to our demands, and ending contemporary society's abundant injustices eludes us. The difference between our moral responsibility and our ability to achieve it infuses left organizing with a permanent sense of panic and disquiet. And our victories, in recent decades, have been few.

Progressive bills die in committee. Legislation becomes watered down as it moves through the system. Radical groups get closer to power, and, as they do, their radicalism is steadily stripped away. Politicians who began to rise in prominence and celebrity as left-wing champions drift toward moderation and working within the system as they are seduced by influence and ambition. Laws that appear transformative when passed prove to be limited in scope and effect when implemented. The youth provide energy, attention, and manpower to the Democratic Party, and they are rewarded time and again with the rule of party hacks who seem doggedly committed to the status quo. The basic logic of the entire edifice of politics, that committed people can use the democratic processes available to them and, over time, craft real change has been disproven again and again. You look out at the world. You see injustice and suffering everywhere. You work to create change. You fail, again and again.

It is hard not to have considerable sympathy for those who are inclined to endorse violence as a tool for achieving left-wing victories. Anyone who has been an organizer for long enough has experienced the profound feelings of hopelessness that real-life politics can engender. And when the injustice seems so deep, the problems so intractable, and the system so indifferent, I can absolutely understand why so many activists often grasp at violence as a solution to their problems. It's the only way they see to, in the words of the Berkeley Free Speech movement pioneer Mario Savio, "put your bodies upon the gears," to make the machinery of injustice stop.

But emotional understanding and strategic endorsement are very different things. While I sympathize with those who feel that they've tried every other method to make the world change, the fact remains that in almost every potential situation faced by left activists in developed countries, the use of violence would prove pointless and counterproductive. The state's monopoly on violence has only grown as technology has progressed and public opinion remains firmly against violent acts. Riots are directionless and burn out quickly. The odds of any type of meaningful victory in combat are laughably low.

NO, RIOTS DON'T "WORK"

During the raging days of 2020, when some protests were breaking out into full-on riots, advocates for the violence (or, at least, defenders of the rioters) trotted out a misremembered quote from a curious source, one that was shared endlessly on social media. The source was Martin Luther

King Jr., the great civil rights icon. The quote was "a riot is the voice of the unheard." The quote was misremembered because King's actual quote was "a riot is the language of the unheard." And the whole thing was curious because the man who said it was a lifelong opponent of riots.

Most of the protests inspired by George Floyd were peaceful. The vast majority of protesters, though filled with righteous and justifiable rage, showed up at the sites of demonstrations, chanted, carried signs, and eventually dispersed. In a few cases, a cop car or two got flipped on its head, and protesters occupied some spaces by force of numbers that the authorities would have preferred remain open. But by and large the protests were remarkably peaceful—not civil, as no protest should be, but peaceful. According to US Crisis Monitor, a project that attempts to quantify political violence in the United States, "In more than 93% of all demonstrations connected to the [Black Lives Matter] movement, demonstrators have not engaged in violence or destructive activity." The report goes on to state that the greatest threat of violence at BLM protests came from the police. (Something true at all protests.) I would not say that this report is a "neutral" source—like seemingly all of our elite institutions, the US Crisis Monitor is thoroughly pro protester—but the report accurately captured the on-the-ground reality of that tense summer. The vast majority of the hundreds of thousands who took to the streets to protest acted peacefully even as they expressed rage.

Perhaps the most common "violent" action was the toppling of statues, most of which had been erected in the honor of Confederate leaders or other historical villains. This provoked a good deal of debate at the time. I can't say I ever felt particularly exercised about any of it; on the one hand, tearing down statues is about as symbolic (and thus empty) as political action can be, but on the other, there really was no reason for our public spaces to honor Confederates in 2020. (The left being the left, this behavior sometimes devolved into self-parody, such as when protesters in Portland, Oregon, set fire to a statue of an elk. Ah, Portland.) I have found no reports of anyone harmed during the tearing down of a statue in 2020. All in all, I can't see how even those rare protests that involved tearing down statues could be considered violent by any fair standard.

Some of the George Floyd protests did devolve into riot behavior, including arson and looting. Some cities saw repeated bouts of protester violence. In places like Minneapolis, Portland, and Seattle, businesses were burned, windows were smashed, stores were looted. The political news outlet Axios estimated that, by September 2020, insurance costs from BLM-related rioting ranged between $1 billion and $2 billion. These actions by a very small percentage of protesters could never undermine the righteousness of the protests, which were a natural and necessary response to a horrific act of police violence. But they did create a bit of a dilemma among a lot of observers on the left: Condemn or condone?

Some alleged that the rioting was the product of false flag operations—that is, that "agent provocateurs" committed acts of violence as a way to undermine the protests. (A notorious case involved "Umbrella Man," a figure seen on video smashing windows in Minneapolis who was later revealed to be a member of the Hells Angels.) I don't doubt that a little of that went on, but I'm also sure that the large majority of rioting behavior didn't stem from these motives. That's not the same as saying that the rioting was the result of dedicated left protestors; protests always attract their fair share of opportunists, some of whom are just looking for an excuse to get violent, and there's no easy way to deal with them. Back during the Iraq War, our protests saw plenty of jerks who just wanted to break things. Protests are public affairs by nature, and you want to be as big of a tent as possible. And most people who show up for them probably do think of themselves as being there for political reasons first, and only devolve into pointless violence if the opportunity arises. You can't judge a protest or protest movement by the actions of a few knuckleheads.

That's part of why I found the ensuing justifications of rioting that popped up in 2020 so aggravating. Many of those who defended rioting were doing so out of a sense of obligation and a general defensiveness toward the protests. Those may be understandable feelings, but they were never necessary: the bad behavior of a few bad actors did nothing to jeopardize the righteousness of the protest movement inspired by the murder of George Floyd. And yet defending riots became something of a cottage industry among progressives in 2020. "Merchandise can be replaced," went one commonplace on social media, "Black lives cannot." Facebook, Twitter, and Instagram were filled with the angry insistence that condemning rioting amounted to "siding with the oppressor." I remember an orthodoxy against criticizing the riots descending on social media that year, an orthodoxy that was enforced with the threat of pile-ons and cancellation.

There was plenty of written fodder to justify this conformity. Author Vicky Osterweil's book *In Defense of Looting* was published in the summer of 2020 but largely written before Floyd's murder. She seized the day, saying in an interview with NPR that riots get "people what they need for free immediately, which means that they are capable of living and reproducing their lives without having to rely on jobs or a wage." As the title of Osterweil's book makes clear, she is not just supportive of protests, or protests that become violent, or of rioting, but of the specific behavior of looters, the stealing that takes advantage of the chaos of a riot. Edgy. Not to be outdone, the wizened liberal magazine *The Nation* published a piece titled "In Defense of Destroying Property," which argued that "too many lines have been crossed, too many innocent people murdered, too many communities over-policed and otherwise neglected to expect anyone to react 'reasonably.'" Why we would want to abandon reason in the face of injustice, I'll never know; this attitude is a good example of the condescension that bloomed in 2020, when many left-leaning people decided that the Floyd protests were too fragile to be treated with adult discrimination and judgment.

Others were more equivocal, taking less of a pro-riot stance than an anti-anti-riot perspective. A piece in *The Atlantic* complained of a double standard, arguing that "only one thing is clear—there is no form of black protest that white supremacy will sanction" and comparing the rioters to those killed in the Boston Massacre. A *National Geographic* photo essay compared the Floyd protests to race riots past, arguing that they "suggest a new phase of opposition that is uniting groups who did not have much in common for most of American history." In *Vox*, it was argued that "civil disobedience is frenzied and chaotic by nature . . . some protesters are looting out of the same anger that drives the protests, and other looters are not protesters at all." The *New York Times* missive in this genre grew florid, arguing that "our country was built on looting—the looting of Indigenous lands and African labor." In fairness, this is not untrue, but perhaps it operates on a level of abstraction so extreme that it provides us with little useful information about whether the Floyd riots were productive. There are many more examples that were published in the year after Floyd's murder. Of course, conservatives also took advantage of the moment; to pick a representative example, a *USA Today* columnist argued that the protests "have given the Second Amendment a boost."

Being pro riot is catnip to a certain sort of person. It's perfect, really: to be pro riot positions yourself as leftier-than-thou, ruffles the feathers of some excitable types, and has almost no connection to any actual real-world political controversy, ensuring that the stakes are low. But this pose collapses with any rigorous application of the question: What do riots actually accomplish?

That quote I referenced before, about riots being the language of the unheard, is indeed a real MLK quote. But its prominence, particularly in 2020, was always weird, and its constant use misleading—opposition to political violence and the uselessness of riots were issues on which King never wavered. Indeed, in one of his last major speeches, known as "A New Sense of Direction," King reiterated his stance: "The limitation of riots, moral questions aside, is that they cannot win, and their participants know it. Hence riots are not revolutionary but reactionary because they invite defeat." This is about as dispositive as it gets and was delivered just a few months before his assassination in April 1968. It represents our best understanding of his thinking at the time of his death. His perspective on riots was withering. "They offer an emotional catharsis," he said, "but they must be followed by a sense of futility."

What strikes me, reading those words today, is how profoundly out of step King would have been with the political environment in 2020. Stripped of their author's name, those words would identify one as a squish, a police apologist, and an implicit supporter of white supremacy. The individual leader most responsible for the most consequential civil rights legislation in our country's history would have been seen as insufficiently radical for the moment.

You'll notice that King thus endorsed the rioter's anger, with his "language of the unheard" comment, but dismissed their tactics. In much of his work, he discussed the moral dimensions of violent resistance, but in "A New Sense of Direction," King fixated on the question of real-world consequences. King was ever and always a radical and would never have greeted cries for justice dismissively. But it's worth pointing out that, if conservatives tend to use King as a pacifist caricature, someone who embraced nonviolence for its own sake rather than as a tool for liberation, those on the left can at times make a similar mistake, failing to understand how relentlessly strategic King was as an activist leader. You can grasp this clearly if you consider the frequent comparisons between Malcolm X and King.

A PRACTICAL UNDERSTANDING OF POLITICAL VIOLENCE

For as long as I can remember, the contrast between Malcolm X and Martin has been used to illustrate broader political dynamics. Often, I've seen the willingness to countenance violence in Malcolm X's rhetoric and the dedication to the peace of King as metonyms for the political extremism of each—the radical Malcolm X and the reformist MLK. Malcolm X was one of the great orators of the twentieth century, and his uncompromising demands for immediate justice were entirely correct on the merits. Few right-minded people could fail to be stirred by the clarity and righteousness of his perspective. But those who see King as some moderate incrementalist counterpart to Malcolm X's radicalism fail in two ways. First, they misunderstand King's own extremism, especially relative to the time; all the demands of his movement, in their era, were radical demands, totally out of keeping with mass opinion and in defiance of many calls for a slower march to progress. Late in his life, King emphasized the labor movement, protested the Vietnam War, and flirted with socialism, demonstrating his left-wing bona fides. More relevant to our purposes here, King was just vastly more effective at achieving change than Malcolm X. This is of course influenced by Malcolm X's tragic assassination, but there's little question that with King's deep influence on historic legislation like the Civil Rights Act and Voting Rights Act, he was a more effective leader. That's not to insult Malcolm X, who was for most of his career saddled with the Nation of Islam (NOI), a fundamentally conservative cultlike religion with a bizarre mythology, and whose post-Nation life was cut short by operatives associated with the NOI. Still, I find the championing of Malcolm X's style of politics over King's, which is common to certain slices of the left, hard to understand.

The key to wading through the question of political violence intelligently is to remain resolutely practical—to once again privilege the material. The debate about when and whether political violence is *justified* is inherently less useful than the question of whether political violence will be *effective*. And, indeed, I think the defenders of left political violence reflexively revert to questions of moral justification because they know questions of practical usefulness will not be answered to their benefit. When the question of left-wing violence or resistance to the state come up, as they often do in radical left spaces, I always ask preliminary questions: What acts? Against what targets? Carried out by whom and how? And to what specific strategic ends? Put more simply: Whom do you propose we hit, how are we going to hit them, and what would be the likely outcome if we do?

The typical response to those questions contains very little in the way of answers and a great deal of resentment. People don't like to answer these questions because they know that if they're answered honestly, the use of political violence will never look wise. What actually existing leftist group maintains the ability to win a meaningful military victory against the state and its forces? I am proud to stand with America's socialists and radicals, warts and all, but we are largely an army of grad students and dreamers. We are not made to engage in combat with anyone, let alone the state.

There is always the sideshow of street fights between antifa and "the fash," leading to the inevitable cadre of slight figures trying to look tough in black hoodies and bandannas at protests. "Antifascism" has a long and complex history, much of it salutary, some of it not. But the positive value of a self-selected group at any protest who has gone there with the intention of engaging in violence is dwarfed by the downsides, which include making things unsafe for other protesters and drawing negative media coverage. Typically, the stated justification for this behavior is that we must be ready to meet the fascists on the street in combat, but many years of experience teaches me that most people who show up wearing all black at protests want to be violent and like having a political justification for doing so. Besides, fistfights at protests are never going to have any significant effect on the political situation, even assuming we win the fights we get into, which we certainly shouldn't assume. Injustice does not reign because of idiot thugs at protests but because of men who put on suits every day and rule over our economy in towers hundreds of feet above the ground. Not one of the "Proud Boys," the laughable proto-fascist organization, could do as much damage in a year as a single Wall Street executive can do in a day. I think people grasp that, at some level, which is why dreams of taking up arms against the whole system still have purchase.

Left history hangs heavy here. Many want to harken back to the great revolutions or resistance movements of the past—1789, 1917, Cuba, the Viet Cong. These were all victories for left-wing causes, though none of those victories were without complication or qualification. But it's essential to understand the differences between the violent revolutions of yore and any potential internal resistance movement in the United States in the twenty-first century. The biggest difference is simply technological change: the establishment military's advantage over any potential revolutionary movement or terrorist cell is vastly greater today than those faced by successful left resistance movements in the past. The Cuban civil war, for example, was mostly fought with rifles and infantry, not the modern machinery and aerial munitions that power contemporary armies. The Russian Revolution took place in a country whose military had been devastated by World War I, famine, and a chronic lack of supplies. It's true that, in Vietnam, the technologically superior Americans proved unable to maintain control of South Vietnam and protect its capitalist government against the Viet Cong and the North. But the Americans faced a restive population at home that was growing more tired of the war by the hour, guerilla tactics that depended on a far greater understanding of the local geography than the American military possessed, and the zeal of people who were fighting to expel a foreign invader from their home. None of that would be true in the event of armed resistance against the current United States government.

Most likely, any attempt to achieve change by force would have no greater influence than the Weathermen, the 1970s leftist terrorist organization that set off some bombs, made a lot of noise, and had zero appreciable effect on American politics. Even if you could amass more followers and gather more guns, the outcome of violence against the state would be predetermined. Consider the military advantage the United States government would hold against any possible internal resistance movement. The first advantage would not be in military might but in intelligence. Revelations about spying by US intelligence agencies, such as those made possible by Edward Snowden, demonstrate that the government would have all the information needed to quell any uprising before it started. Anytime members of a resistance group used a cell phone, their communications could be easily intercepted; simply having the device on in their pocket would enable the state to track them. Movement of vehicles or ordnance would be even more easily trackable. The FBI would likely infiltrate any group, sending in clandestine agents to engage in surveillance and sow discord. And those are mere intelligence advantages; the advantage in the use of force enjoyed by the state would be massive, far greater than that enjoyed by establishment governments that were defeated by famous historical resistance movements. A left resistance movement would likely be operating almost entirely with assault rifles and homemade bombs, while the state would meet them with tanks, MRAPs (mine-resistant ambush-protected vehicles), bombers that can hit a target from so far away they can't be seen, Predator drones. The state has satellites that can read your T-shirt from space. You cannot possibly defeat the American system with force of arms. The idea is absurd.

So absurd that I'm sure many readers are wondering why I'm bothering to waste time on this topic. But I have spent enough time in left spaces to know how often the idea of armed resistance rolls around, wasting time, every time. If nothing else, I feel compelled to make the basic argument against this folly here because I never want to have to make it again. The romance of armed struggle has sucked in too many passionate organizers, taking time away from the boring, quotidian work of making change. Defenses of protest violence and rioting are not the same thing as endorsements of larger campaigns of violent resistance to the state, yet they share an underlying emotionality and the feeling of grasping at straws. I take time to enumerate the senselessness of both because they so often crowd out the sensible in radical left conversation. I suspect that part of the confusion in this debate stems from the assumption that rejecting political violence leaves us only with the system, with the partisan politics that seem so corrupt and broken to so many. But, again, the example of Martin Luther King Jr. is illustrative. King achieved legislative victories, and those victories represent some of the biggest advances in the history of American civil rights. But King and his organizations used a variety of tactics throughout his career, including acts of civil disobedience that resulted in King's arrest. Indeed, the legislative victories of the mid-1960s only became possible because of the direct action of innumerable activists, much of it illegal. The night before his assassination, King gave his last speech, in the support of striking sanitation workers in Memphis; strikes are not a part of the conventional partisan political system but a form of direct action. The options are not either political violence or deference to the Democrats and business as usual. We have more tools than that.

THE WILL OF THE PEOPLE

There's another reason that armed resistance is likely to fail in a developed nation in the contemporary world, and certainly the United States, other than the practical folly of trying to fight against state forces, and this reason is even more touchy for many leftists: the people lack the will necessary to support a resistance movement. Their conditions are not like the conditions faced by the citizens of countries where left revolutionary movements have succeeded. Our problems are immense, but they tend to be less acute than those that inspired those historical movements.

Let me be clear: There is ample reason for twenty-first-century Americans to feel political unrest, even political rage. Our political system is defined by gridlock and dysfunction, our culture by a holy war between liberals and conservatives, and our economy by rampant and entrenched inequality. Throughout the country, poor people live desperate lives, clinging to whatever small material gains they can scratch out, getting by on disability payments for phony back injuries, addicted to OxyContin. My entire worldview is based on my belief that our system is rotten, and that a better world, a far better world, is possible, right now. I bow to no one in my belief in the desperate need for change.

But capitalism provides abundance along with abundant injustice. Indeed, the dark genius of our system lies in its ability to pacify even as it exploits. Americans ground down under the heel of the system very often do not direct their anger back at that system. Too many Americans today who might take up the fight against the establishment have been bought off by $2 cheeseburgers, opioids, video games, and internet porn. This isn't to blame them for their own condition, which is the fault of our government, our economic system, and our elites. It's simply to point out that the average American has more to risk than those people who took up with Lenin, with Castro, with Ho Chi Minh. When I look at the history of successful revolutionary movements of the past, I see countries of vast need in the most basic elements of human life.

Consider the Russian Revolution of 1917. The establishment czarist government was a model of ineptitude and dysfunction. The system was totally autocratic, a decaying monarchy that had virtually no room for input by the public at large. The economic system was a shambles, as the government's witless attempts at modernization had left the great majority of the country undeveloped and unable to take advantage of the material abundance that the industrial revolution had provided in other countries. As a result, Russia was still a primarily agricultural society, with a large peasant population and a small industrial sector. Serfs lived in poverty and were oppressed by the feudal system. Famines had left many common people literally starving. All of this resulted in widespread inequality and discontent among the working class.

Unsurprisingly, then, there were myriad political groups and movements within Russia that opposed czarist rule; eventually, they would turn against each other for control of the country. But Russia was gripped with hatred for the establishment government, creating a welcoming environment for a group like the Bolsheviks. And while Americans suffer under immense rent burdens and from the depravities of a broken health care system, few risk actually starving to death, as has been true in many countries where revolutionary change was achieved. What's more, while American democracy is deeply imperfect, there is at least some degree of community control of government, of democratic rule. In country after country that has seen revolution, this has not been the case. Cubans suffered under the despotic control of Fulgencio Batista, Iranians under the corrupt and brutal shah, Vietnamese under foreign occupation and an illegitimate puppet government. The conditions that made these places ripe for revolutionary movements simply are not seen in twenty-first-century developed nations.

I think the United States should see major structural change to its economic and political systems. I think its people are hungry for a better deal. And I think that there are many other effective avenues to achieving political change than dutifully lining up to vote every two or four years. There are alternatives to working within the same corrupt system. But while change of a revolutionary character is possible, it's only possible through persuading enough people to our cause and achieving change through democratic means. No great American revolution is coming in the early twenty-first century. We have to accept the frustrations and insufficient pace of doing things the old-fashioned way. That will mean, unfortunately, going slowly when justice demands speed, accepting less than what we want when what we want is reasonable and right, working with people we would prefer to avoid, and accepting that being right and doing good are very different things. This isn't an endorsement of moderation, or even of incrementalism, if we understand those ideas properly. We can be radical in both demand and method, but we cannot be self-deluded about the lessons of history. We can hold Malcolm X in our hearts and Martin Luther King in our heads. I have complicated feelings about the legacy of Che Guevara, but there can be no complication in understanding his ultimate end: dead in the jungle, his campaign for Bolivian liberation an abject failure.

I've said that we must be resolutely practical when evaluating tactics, and that's what political violence is, a set of tactics. For Fidel Castro and Che in the 1950s, squatting in the Cuban jungle as they fought against a corrupt and cruel government, such violence proved to be a very effective tactic indeed. A decade later, it failed Che in Bolivia. Tactics are always contextual. For those of us on the left in the contemporary United States, practicality will always have some relationship to popularity. We don't have to slavishly devote ourselves to what's already popular; if we did, we would have no left program at all. But we do have to pay attention to where the public is now, and to where we want to take them, at all times. We can't give up on core goals—like a dramatically more open immigration policy—simply because those goals are currently unpopular. But since violence is always a tactic and never an end itself, the popularity of political violence is tantamount to its value—if we commit acts of political violence in pursuit of some end, but erode our popularity in doing so, we are at best running in place.

And we can say with considerable confidence that political violence is not popular in the United States. In a 2022 poll, only about 20 percent of poll respondents felt that the use of violence was appropriate to achieve a political goal. Another poll from Reuters/Ipsos found that only 17 percent of Americans believe political violence is sometimes acceptable against one's political enemy. And the polling analysis site FiveThirtyEight argued that even these numbers were likely inflated by problematically worded questions. On the subject of the Black Lives Matter riots specifically, one 2021 poll found that two-thirds of polled Americans wanted congressional investigations into those incidents. We might take these findings with a grain of salt, given that the poll was commissioned by the National Police Association. But a similar 2020 poll found that, while large majorities were sympathetic to the peaceful protests, only 22 percent felt that violence and unrest were an appropriate response to George Floyd's death.

Protests have many purposes. Sometimes, they exist only to ensure that attention is paid to a great injustice so that no one can later say that a historic crime passed unnoticed. But the summer of 2020 was different. Public attention had been captured to an unprecedented degree, and there was such an outpouring of outrage and solidarity with protesters that persuasion and possibility were at the forefront of everyone's mind. Few could have predicted that a moment like that would lead to so little tangible police reform. The forces of reaction were always going to find an excuse not to support sensible reforms. And at a crucial moment, too

many righteous protests devolved into the directionless and counterproductive behavior of riots. Those riots were not the sole or even primary
reason why so little was accomplished in the wake of the Floyd protests.
But they muddied the waters when it was most important that our purpose remain clear. They certainly didn't help; they almost certainly hurt.
And for what? The fantasy of deliverance through violence is one the left
can't afford to entertain anymore.

4

THE NONPROFIT INDUSTRIAL COMPLEX

What sort of thoughtless person would criticize the nonprofit sector? In a sea of capitalist greed, they work for higher purposes. Tax breaks associated with giving to nonprofit institutions induce the wealthy to spread some of their wealth. An army of idealists has found employment at nonprofit institutions that allow them to work for something more than a paycheck. What could there be to criticize in all of that?

Plenty, as it turns out. There are, to pick some prominent examples, questions about the efficiency of nonprofits' use of funds, about accountability and transparency of their leadership, about their dependence on deep-pocketed funders and the potential for inappropriate influence, and about their fundamental elitism and disconnection from the average citizen. They have a particularly malign influence on the left because they cannibalize the energy and purpose of our movements. Passionate radicals find themselves in the nonprofit pipeline and end up neutered and buried under paperwork. And yet for decades, nonprofit groups have been the organizing forces of local activism across a vast range of geographies and causes. We can't understand how the contemporary left functions without understanding the nonprofit industrial complex.

"Nonprofit" is an umbrella term that, in an American context, usually refers to an entity that enjoys a special legal status that exempts it from most taxes. These organizations operate under certain regulatory constraints (a point to which we will return) and are "nonprofit" in the sense that no person or entity is meant to become enriched by them (a point to which we will also return). There are a variety of designations in the tax code for such organizations, such as Section 501(c)(5), which includes labor unions, and Section 501(c)(4), for social welfare organizations, homeowners associations, and volunteer fire companies. One of the most common, and most consequential, is Section 501(c)(3), the public charities. A nonprofit dedicated to saving the mountain gorilla that collects charitable contributions from gorilla lovers, pays for staff and overhead, and distributes its revenues in a manner designed to help save the gorillas is a 501(c)(3). For practical purposes, a 501(c)(4) can act in more directly political ways than a 501(c)(3), while donations to a 501(c)(3) are usually tax deductible, where donations to a 501(c)(4) are not.

It's easy to underestimate just how big the nonprofit sector is. According to the Urban Institute's National Center for Charitable Statistics, in 2019 approximately one and a half *million* nonprofits were registered with the IRS in the United States. Their collective spending that year was more than one trillion dollars and accounted for 5.5 percent of US gross domestic product (GDP). This is an immense amount of economic activity. For contrast, according to the National Center for Education Statistics, American K–12 education made up only 3.5 percent of GDP in 2018. According to the National Council of Nonprofits, an organization that advocates for nonprofits—itself a nonprofit, naturally—there are almost 150,000 registered nonprofit organizations in California alone.

Some of this size is attributable to groups like pension funds and volunteer fire companies, which are not really what most people think of when they talk about nonprofits. Still, there is an enormous number of charitable nonprofit organizations in the United States, and the sector is only growing. Between 2007 and 2016, for example, the increase in nonprofit employment outpaced the increase in for-profit employment by three to one. By the end of that period, the nonprofit sector was the third-largest employer in the entire country in terms of total wages—larger than finance, retail, and food service. This is an immensely influential part of our society, yet public interest in it appears low.

Nonprofits play a disproportionate role in our political apparatus, our educational systems, and our basic civic functioning, but most Americans putter along without pausing to think too much about them. Indeed, defining the purpose of the nonprofit sector would likely be difficult for most Americans. In part this stems from the nature of nonprofits—from their very not-for-profit nature. Sure, they pull in a great deal of public funding, but because most nonprofit money is donated, many of us see little reason to give the fair and efficient use of that money a harsh accounting. Yet a sector that comprises 5.5 percent of our national GDP demands intense scrutiny, for its sheer size if nothing else.

In arguing against the outsize influence of nonprofit organizations, I'm swimming against the tide of public opinion. The National Council of Nonprofits defines the sector of the economy that it advocates for in, shall we say, elevated terms:

> Charitable nonprofits embody the best of America. They provide a
> way for people to work together for the common good, transforming
> shared beliefs and hopes into action. They give shape to our boldest
> dreams, highest ideals, and noblest causes. America's 1.3 million charitable nonprofits feed, heal, shelter, educate, inspire, enlighten, and

nurture people of every age, gender, race, and socioeconomic status, from coast to coast, border to border, and beyond. They foster civic engagement and leadership, drive economic growth, and strengthen the fabric of our communities. Every single day.

This is hyperbole, yes, but it also reflects a broader public understanding of the nonprofit industry. Most people have faith that the sector works for the betterment of society. A 2021 study found that research consistently reflects broad public support for nonprofits. It cited a 2009 paper that found that most of the public feels that nonprofits make good decisions (76 percent), run programs and services wisely (76 percent), and spend money appropriately (61 percent).

Still, there's no shortage of criticisms of the nonprofit industrial complex; indeed, the term itself is something of a cliché. Left discursive spaces are rife with writers, journalists, and activists who disdain the nonprofit sector's influence on our efforts. But because they are so large, so loosely regulated, and so little understood, it's imperative to understand why they sometimes operate as a negative force for progressive causes, dragging us down as a political movement. First though, we need to attend to the problems with nonprofits that anyone might agree on, regardless of political leanings.

THE GENERAL CASE AGAINST NONPROFITS

The first major complaint we might level against the nonprofit sector is its lack of transparency and accountability. These institutions suck up public funds and fulfill essential societal functions, and yet their basic internal processes are often entirely opaque. The nonprofit community at least acknowledges the importance of transparency and accountability in general. "America's charitable nonprofits rely on the public trust to do their work and advance their missions," says the National Council of Nonprofits website, which "is why it is so important that charitable nonprofits continuously earn the public's trust through their commitment to ethical principles, transparency, and accountability." Yet many perceive that the average nonprofit is falling down on the job when it comes to transparency. A 2015 paper by Barry D. Friedman and Amanda M. Wolcott is withering in this regard. "Such preferences [for confidentiality], of course, may be directed toward the majority members' own personal interests," they write. "Confidentiality, therefore, is more likely to protect their personal interests rather than any societal interests." Nonprofits all have a legal duty to be somewhat transparent with their funds, and some states (such as California) expand on these responsibilities. All nonprofits must make available three years' worth of IRS form 990-T, which details some aspects of nonprofit spending. Yet these forms do little to reassure the public about the efficient use of funds, and in many ways the average nonprofit remains a black box.

If you're asking people for money based on the pretext that you'll be using it for a good cause, it's essential for those who are giving you that money to feel confident that their donations will actually serve that cause. Yet again and again in my research, I encountered great cynicism about the public's ability to know how such funds are spent. And this sense of throwing money into a hole has increased exponentially as internet technologies have made donation effortless. "The role of nonprofits in helping people act as problem solvers for the causes they care about can only be sustained with sufficient [donor] trust in that relationship," wrote Alina Clough, a fellow at George Mason University's Mercatus Center, "but the ease with which donations can be given means that legitimacy is not always clear." When donating was a harder, more time-consuming process, donors to nonprofits had greater incentive to investigate precisely where their money was going, but with the effort involved in donating dropping to near zero, thanks to seamless internet donation, so too drops basic discrimination about spending money wisely. "Recipients of donations can range from questionable to outright fraudulent," wrote Clough.

It's difficult to arrive at a quantitative metric to assess what proportion of nonprofits practice adequate transparency practices, both because it's hard to define transparency in quantitative terms and because so few organizations are, well, transparent about their practices. A later paper by Friedman and Wolcott looked at eighty-five charities in Georgia. As a proxy for overall openness, they asked that these organizations share their most recent minutes from meetings of the boards of directors. Little more than a third of these organizations did so, and a majority did not provide audited financial statements. One would think that information on the basic operations of a board of trustees and minimal financial openness would not be too much to ask for. The authors concluded, "Countless leaders of nonprofit organizations can read this paper and a library full of books and journals advocating transparency, and they will be unmoved by them and continue to assert their privilege to shroud their operations in secrecy."

Another common and related criticism lies in the inefficiency of nonprofits and the way they spend their funds. The watchdog organization Charity Navigator estimates that seven out of ten charities have a "program efficiency ratio" of at least 75 percent. A program efficiency ratio involves dividing a nonprofit's amount spent on programs by its total expenses so that a program efficiency ratio of 50 percent would indicate that half of every donated dollar went to the specific charitable programs of the organization. Of course, this invites the inevitable question of what counts as a program expense, a metric that sounds easy to game. Unfortunately, philanthropic (in)efficiency is also hard to quantify due to various accounting quirks—some of them no doubt engineered by the organizations themselves. A 2008 report by the nonprofit consultancy

Bridgespan Group admitted, "It's a badly kept secret that overhead costs in the nonprofit sector are most often much greater than what's visible in financial reports and fundraising literature."

The American Red Cross, one of the largest charitable organizations in the world, boasts that it spends 88 percent of its budget on "program services." Is this good? It sounds reasonable to me. But drilling down complicates matters. For example, the biggest part of the Red Cross's budget is biomedical services. More than half of that money is spent on employee salaries and benefits—that is, on the salaries of the people who administer those biomedical services. Is *that* good? On the one hand, it seems entirely appropriate to me for such an organization to spend a lot on staffing. On the other hand, employee salaries are frequently considered part of overhead costs and thus something to be minimized to the extent possible. It's very difficult to tell what efficiency precisely means for a nonprofit, and this is part of the essential difficulty of philanthropic giving: deciding where to give depends on knowledge the average person doesn't have and value judgments they're ill-equipped to make.

The world of "effective altruism," a group of like-minded people who doggedly look for the best possible use of charitable funds, evolved precisely because of frustration with the inefficient use of charitable donations. The organization GiveWell, which directs potential donors to organizations that they see as unusually efficient in terms of achieving altruistic ends like saving lives, is frequently cited as a model of effective altruism. And their origin story depends entirely on the inefficiency and lack of transparency of traditional nonprofit charities. "GiveWell started when a group of friends asked how their charitable donations could accomplish as much good as possible," their website reads, "[and] found that information to answer that question was not available through existing donor resources, or even directly from charities." GiveWell's definitions of what constitutes effective giving are certainly debatable—indeed,

I find them quite tendentious, such as their indifference toward any programming regarding the arts or other human enrichment—but the fact that such an organization exists speaks volumes as to the efficiency of the average charity. Charity Navigator also works to provide as much information to potential donors as possible, again driven by both a lack of openness among nonprofits and an impression of misspent funds in the industry. Charity Navigator has traditionally brought a lot of focus to bear on overhead and waste, while GiveWell tends to focus more on ultimate effectiveness. But both demonstrate dissatisfaction with charitable giving as conventionally practiced.

Of course nonprofits need to spend some money on office space, supplies, salaries for workers, and other elements that any organization requires. But every dollar spent inefficiently is a dollar not spent on a given cause.

And it's not merely the poor use of funding at issue; it's the question of the quid pro quo, of whose needs a nonprofit should ultimately serve. You would think that people within the nonprofit world would at least pay lip service to the idea that, ultimately, these organizations must serve those they identify as the beneficiaries of their charity and programs. I'd expect such messaging to be universal, for optics if nothing else. And yet an extraordinary document from the National Association of Nonprofit Organizations & Executives lays out in stark language that this simply isn't true.

At the end of the day, for nonprofit organizations—Money is more important than Mission. Nonprofits exist to serve and to meet needs on a global scale, and we care deeply for the causes we embrace, often to the detriment of our funders. A successful nonprofit knows that their #1 Customer is their donors, period. Without the donors, there would be no impact, no people served, no mouths fed, no backs clothed. Those we serve are important, but if we really want to have an impact, we must take care of our donors first, we must make sure that our programs are designed to give our donors an opportunity to fulfill the goals they have for their philanthropy.

I assure you that this is a real passage from a major organization in the nonprofit world and that I have not robbed it of context inappropriately. It appears that some in that space really do believe that philanthropy should be a service industry and the donors, the customers. Of course, as the quoted text makes clear, the actual intended beneficiary of treating donors as the primary target in philanthropy is the nonprofits and their employees themselves—donors are important to the degree to which they keep the lights on at a given nonprofit. This is a core criticism of nonprofits, and one of the most cutting, that ultimately their function is to remain in business so that the employees who run them continue to have jobs.

The early-twentieth-century Italian sociologist Robert Michels developed what he called "the iron law of oligarchy," which argued that over time, any human organization would develop an internal elite that worked for their own best interest to consolidate power and protect their position. A nonprofit organization can be a great example of Michels's law at work: while ostensibly dedicated to a specific charitable mission, over time the interests of those in power within the organization will crowd out that mission in favor of protecting leadership. It's hardly unusual for workers within a given institution to put too much of a premium on keeping the bosses happy. But without the organizing force of the profit motive, the temptation to do what satisfies the ruling oligarchy of a given nonprofit is even greater than in a for-profit institution.

In a similar vein, in 2007, the blogger Jon Schwarz developed "the iron law of institutions," which holds that "the people who control institutions care first and foremost about *their power within the institution* rather than the *power of the institution itself.*" That is to say, if you look at actually existing human institutions, people within them don't do things that would make the institutions more healthy but jeopardize their own place within the institution. You can imagine a vice president of a company who heads up his own division. Over time, he becomes convinced that his division is wasteful and unnecessary and that it could be dissolved, with its functions folded into other divisions. What Schwarz argues is that such a person would never bring this opinion to the rest of his company's leadership, because while doing so would make the institution more efficient, it would also jeopardize his own stature within the institution. I believe that this dynamic plays out very often in nonprofit organizations; the prosecution of a nonprofit's ostensible mission is always going to be secondary to the continued functioning of the organization. People don't make their own jobs obsolete.

Consider a nonprofit that has a very specific problem to address, such as the eradication of a given disease. This isn't hard to imagine; we can point to the eradication of smallpox in 1980 as an example. The question becomes, what would a nonprofit dedicated to fighting a disease do if that disease was eradicated? The most socially beneficial thing might be to close their doors so that the money spent on that organization can find more useful causes. But how many organizations would have the integrity to do so, rather than finding some way to pivot in how they define their mission? HIV and AIDS are not solved problems, obviously, particularly in underdeveloped countries. But a cure and vaccine no longer seem like science fiction. What will the dozens and dozens of nonprofits associated with fighting HIV and AIDS do once the disease is defeated?

It's a long-standing critique of nonprofits, that they must appear to be addressing social problems without actually solving them, for fear of destroying their own reason for existing. As a piece by the news service collective Common Dreams once put it, "The purpose of the nonprofit sector writ large is not to solve social problems—it is to perpetuate them."

I suspect that this is why so many nonprofit organizations have vague and general mission statements: the less obvious their role, the more they can evolve their purpose over time. The large American nonprofit network the United Way has such an opaque purpose that they used to run television ads making fun of that fact.

Finally, nonprofits are subject to complaints about elitism and lack of representation. A common complaint is that the people who work for nonprofits do not look like the communities they serve. Sevetri Wilson, the founder of a technology company that develops platforms for nonprofit organizations, wrote in 2020, "There isn't just a lack of BIPOC representation in nonprofits—there are also rooted inequities that determine which organizations receive funding and the level of support they can expect over time." This is a boilerplate complaint about charitable organizations that work in high-poverty areas; the specter of the clueless white do-gooder descending on a community of color looms large. But the problem is acute in nonprofits' leadership. A 2017 survey from the firm Battalia Winston found that 87 percent of nonprofit executive directors were white. While the ranks of lower-level nonprofit workers are surely more diverse and organizations that are dominantly white and higher-educated can no doubt still do good work, it's bad optics for a sector of the labor force that so often works in poor communities of color. It will come as no surprise that nonprofits are routinely accused of being out of touch with the actual needs of low-income people.

Those are all conventional arguments about nonprofit organizations that are, more or less, nonpartisan. For me, the deeper issues are specific to a left perspective, and the lost promise of 2020 provides a good reason as to why.

THE LEFT CASE AGAINST NONPROFITS

Critiques of the nonprofit sector from the right are not uncommon. Those on the right complain that nonprofits as a whole function as tax-free vehicles for liberalism and as a wing of the Democratic Party. In 2019, for example, *Wall Street Journal* columnist Kimberley A. Strassel argued that, despite common liberal complaints about "dark interests" impacting American politics, the most obvious such interests are nonprofits that advocate for liberal causes. In similar terms, the conservative writer and now Ohio senator J. D. Vance claimed in *Newsweek* in 2021 that organizations like the Ford Foundation, which controls some $16 billion in assets, receive special tax status while ultimately serving only Democratic ends. "Left-wing activism pays very well, it turns out," wrote Vance, "so long as it's packaged as charity."

Little firm information exists on the partisan or ideological makeup of nonprofits, which isn't hard to understand; for most such organizations, openly identifying with a particular party would only invite scrutiny and hassle. It's therefore impossible to assign specific percentages to determine how left- or right-leaning the nonprofit sector is as a whole. Few would question, however, that many of the best funded and most powerful nonprofits are ideologically progressive. For one thing, most who work at nonprofit agencies are college-educated, and college graduates tend to be left-leaning. Nonprofits also tend to be concerned with helping the poor and disenfranchised as part of their basic missions, and work on issues of poverty and inequality has an inherent progressive slant. Do-gooders lean left.

The progressive "bias" of the nonprofit sector doesn't bother me much because, well, I'm a leftist. If these agencies advance a left agenda, I welcome it. My issue is that, while most of these organizations may have progressive sympathies and progressive staffers, their effects in the world are often contrary to the left's goals.

Let's begin with the money. Far too many institutions are fixated on accumulating funds in a way that obscures their actual goals—ironically nonprofits become too invested in the profit motive. For example, a *Fast Company* article from 2018 detailed multiple complaints that the Silicon Valley Community Foundation, a nonprofit beloved of many in the tech sector, was sitting on billions. Though I'm not really talking about colleges and universities in this chapter, such institutions are a perfect example of entities that receive special tax status thanks to their supposedly not-for-profit status and then greedily hoard money. At the time of this writing Harvard's endowment is more than $40 billion. Sometimes, this emphasis on revenue generation serves the purpose of overpaying the people who raise the money; in 2012 the *Fiscal Times* published a top-ten list of "Insanely Overpaid Nonprofit Execs," all of whom made in the millions of dollars. But the problem isn't really hoarding wealth or overpaying staff; the problem is that, over time, raising funds becomes the end instead of the means. Chasing donors becomes the central obsession of nonprofits.

A good summary of this problem was articulated in 2013 by Sue Gardner, who served as executive director of the Wikimedia Foundation (the nonprofit that oversees Wikipedia) and has years of experience in the nonprofit space. It's worth quoting her at length.

> Every nonprofit has two main jobs: you need to do your core work, and you need to make the money to pay for it. . . .
>
> Nonprofits also prioritize revenue. But for most it doesn't actually serve as much of an indicator of overall effectiveness. . . . That means that most, or often all, the actual experiences a donor has with a nonprofit are related to fundraising, which means that over time many nonprofits have learned that the donating process needs—in

and of itself—to provide a satisfying experience for the donor. All sorts of energy is therefore dedicated towards making it exactly that: donors get glossy newsletters of thanks, there are gala dinners, they are elaborately consulted on a variety of issues, and so forth.

This means that inside most of nonprofitland—and unique to nonprofitland—there's a structural problem of needing to provide positive experiences for donors that is disconnected from the core work of the organization. This has a variety of unintended effects, all of which undermine effectiveness. Donors bring in money, but wooing donors costs money. Spending those funds is not always inappropriate, if the amount raised in turn is sufficient. But major nonprofits over time can become fancy dinner factories, spending so much time and effort on cozying up to the rich and influential that their actual charitable mission is marginalized. The reality is that, given the internal incentives of these organizations, the best fundraiser will likely rise higher and faster in an organization than the staffer most dedicated to the nonprofit's actual mission. The general claim that nonprofits have an unhealthy dedication to gathering funds rather than spending them effectively is widespread. But it's worth focusing on Gardner's proffered reason: the donors are the ultimate stakeholders for a nonprofit's spending, not those who would ostensibly receive its help, and the donors are rarely aware of the on-the-ground realities of the populations the nonprofits serve.

The issues with attracting donors go beyond sucking up resources and looking untoward: the tax break dangled in front of potential donors invites its own qualms. A fundamental concern with charitable donations to nonprofits is that those donations are usually tax-deductible. Indeed, a huge part of the basic appeal that nonprofits make to potential donors is the ability to earn a tax break—which can look an awful lot like robbing Peter to pay Paul.

One man's tax break is another man's reduced tax revenues. It's very common for the wealthy to see nonprofit donations as a way to stick it to the taxman; they might be giving their money away, but at least they aren't giving it to the government. All of that money that's therefore not taxed is money that fails to end up on the government balance sheet, reducing the availability of public funds for public uses—public uses like the many programs and institutions that the left advocates for. By taking money that would eventually find its way into the tax system and putting it into the hands of an army of private organizations, the nonprofit industrial complex drains the public coffers and reduces public accountability. Tax breaks mean that charitable giving isn't just a well-meaning pastime of the wealthy; they mean that the nonprofit system functions as a drain on the public sector. Surely the wealthy would find tax dodges for some of the money that they donate were there no charitable giving tax incentive, but still the amount of money denied to the public coffers is massive. Here, I would remind you of the immense size of the nonprofit sector.

It's essential to understand the degree to which nonprofits have taken on burdens that once were and still should be relegated to the public sector. In many key areas of American life, functions that were once performed by government (and thus at least theoretically subject to public influence) have been taken on by nonprofit organizations. "Indeed," wrote Jeffrey M. Berry and David F. Arons in *A Voice for Nonprofits*, "the modern welfare state has largely been subcontracted to nonprofits." And that's bad! It's bad because, as progressive people, we should want a vibrant and expansive public sector. Offloading functions that government should provide, such as the provisioning of shelter, health care, and education, removes those services from democratic control and contributes to the withering of the social welfare state. Replacing public governance and investment with unaccountable private organizations and their bureaucracies has a name: neoliberalism.

The INCITE! Collective, a national activist organization of radical feminist women of color, published a book-length attack on the nonprofit industrial complex in 2017. They located nonprofits within the neoliberal turn of the past half century, arguing that nonprofits now play roles once reserved for public services and in so doing help prevent public agitation for expansion and improvement of such public services. They also alleged that nonprofits help to perpetuate the myth of the deserving and undeserving poor.

"With their funding restrictions and a social service model of targeted constituents," they wrote, "non-profits may reproduce categories of deserving and undeserving along lines of legible and illegible identities in the communities on whose behalf the state calls on them to speak." That is to say, nonprofit dollars are almost always distributed in such a way as to distinguish some select group as specially deserving of their generosity, an act which inherently creates an implied class of the undeserving. And this undermines a core tenet of left philosophy, which is that basic human needs such as food, clothing, shelter, education, and health care are not privileges that must be earned but rights that accrue to each of us by dint of being human. Thanks to their funding mandates and the moral assumptions of their funders, nonprofits almost always come with "deserves" strings attached, even if their targeted population is "the most needy"—an inherently political, value-laden concept. It's particularly the case in the post-2020 landscape that nonprofits are likely to seek to serve racial or gender minorities, thanks to the ideologies of their staffers and the incentives of grant writing. But if philanthropy is taking on roles better handled by the state, and philanthropic organizations are increasingly apt to chop the world up into the deserving and the not, who provides essential universal benefits?

The criticism of nonprofits that's most relevant to the broader themes of this book is of the role of nonprofits in left organizing. After two decades of work in various organizing capacities, I can say that nonprofit organizations are both essential to the basic operations of left-wing activism and a drag on its ambitions and radicalism.   .

My formative experiences as an activist, during the anti–Iraq War movement, didn't involve a lot of work with nonprofit organizations. Antiwar groups tend to be much looser and more skeptical affairs. ANSWER (Act Now to Stop War and End Racism), which functioned as something like a steering committee for the antiwar movement of the aughts—for better and, mostly, for worse—now has an affiliated 501(3)(c), but it's unclear when that arrangement started. (ANSWER's role in anti–Iraq War activism and the endlessly bubbling controversies over their influence would take another book to unpack.) The groups I ran around with were fly-by-night affairs mostly; just collections of people who decided to get together and crowd into someone's living room or the offices of a friendly union local after-hours.

If that sounds romantic—and these memories are quite romantic for me—I'm afraid I have bad news. While informal organizing and seat-of-your-pants activism will always be part of left political practice, there are severe limits to this kind of approach. Without formal leadership, there's little accountability; without professional responsibility, little gets done; and without some sort of formal structure, there are no resources. Many of the antiwar efforts I witnessed were hamstrung by a perpetual lack of money—money for buses to transport protesters to distant events, money for signs and shirts, money for porta-potties at protests. There was also, often enough, a conspicuous lack of prior coordination about how to deal with arrests. That essential function would typically be effectively pawned off on nonprofits: groups like the National Lawyers Guild, a bar association of lefty lawyers who defend dissidents and protesters. The anti–Iraq War movement never really "worked," in a certain sense, but to the degree that it did, its many structureless groups were backstopped by a smaller number of formal organizations, most of them nonprofits.

In my work in housing activism, in contrast, I see nonprofit organizations everywhere. Many of the most prominent tenant rights groups in New York City are formally recognized with nonprofit status. The group that I personally organize with has both 501(c)(3) and 501(c)(4) arms, to give them flexibility in terms of the kind of programming they can administer. (Recall that 501(c)(3)s have certain restrictions on political activity, such as endorsing candidates for office, while 501(c)(4)s do not.) Such groups have at least a few full-time staffers, which means that there are people whose job it is to do the basic bureaucratic work of organizing. It's easier to engender responsibility when groups are formal and defined by a set leadership structure, even when a given task is being performed by a volunteer. Local politicians are more ready to listen to groups that have legal recognition, and it's easier to get in the door with various stakeholders. It's hard to imagine the New York housing movement as I know it without the structure and support of nonprofits.

So, what's my complaint? Organization and formal legal recognition are double-edged swords. It's true that nonprofits can be more reliable, more responsible, and better resourced than less "official" groups. It's also true that nonprofits can be overly cautious, mired in internal bureaucracy, structurally inclined toward centrism, and extraordinarily risk-averse. Nonprofits have executive leadership structures and boards of trustees, and thus many potential veto points within their decision-making apparatus. With so many stakeholders who can effectively end any initiative, many good ideas go unimplemented. And by being the groups with the most formal and legal recognition involved with a given action, they also can make the most attractive targets for legal action. Nonprofit employees are keenly aware of this dynamic and many have a tendency to be the people at protests saying, "Let's not get too crazy." They are the ones likely to have to answer for any trouble, and there's an inherent relationship between organization and risk intolerance; if you're invested enough to have done the groundwork of building a nonprofit, you're also invested enough to be defensive about what you've built.

As Paul Klein wrote in *Stanford Social Innovation Review*, "At a time when we need change more than ever, too many nonprofits are constrained by a slow-moving, institutional, and self-interested model."

It's important to note here that this line of criticism has nothing to do with the leftist bona fides of individuals who work for left-leaning nonprofits. Indeed, many of the nonprofit workers I've known have been very committed radicals. But this is precisely the point: nonprofits tend to be *staffed* by leftists and *structurally* conservative. They avoid risk because risk can undermine the continuing operations of the organizations. They resist change because implementing change can result in reprisals from authority within a given nonprofit. They avoid direct action and extralegal means because they have their special tax status to protect. The nonprofit sector's conservatism isn't about the people but about the nature of all institutions. It's also about the power of inertia; as Klein noted, "Many charities are mired in an old approach to social change that is also reflected in how they raise funds."

The idea of a deep state has become a culture-war football in recent years, but there is no doubt that there is a layer of administrative employees within the government who do not change during transfers from one presidential administration to another and who influence the progress of American democracy. Washington has many, many permanent employees who are unelected and yet whose actions have serious consequences for our country. That was the original concept of the "deep state." Well— nonprofits are the deep state of American political activism. They have influence beyond their numbers, they can direct the course of broad movements that should rightfully be led by volunteer organizers, and they pull those movements toward incrementalism and working within the system regardless of the radicalism of their employees. The deficiencies of the nonprofit model are a particularly bad fit for radical-left organizing, as the left calls for big change, now. I'm sure a centrist nonprofit organization finds the bureaucracy and administrivia of such groups to be a cozy fit. For those people fighting for systemic change, for entirely different social paradigms, the conservative tendencies of legally recognized nonprofits can be deadly.

And about those nonprofit employees. I will never blame people for being so invested in organizing and philanthropy that they seek to do so full-time, and everyone deserves the ability to pay the rent. The trouble isn't that people are getting paid to be organizers. The trouble is that, thanks to the organizational incentives of nonprofits and the intrinsic risk-aversion of institutions, the nonprofit hiring cycle takes radical activists and turns them into overworked functionaries. Again, this isn't an indictment of anyone's character, just an observation about the structural realities of organizations.

The people who are most aware of this dynamic are the employees themselves. I can't tell you how many people from nonprofits I've met who remain deeply committed to their causes, are generally proud of the organizations they work for, and yet have developed a deep cynicism. Often these are people who graduated from college with big ideas about turning the system upside down. Getting a job working for a nonprofit that could pay the rent (preferably in a cool city) was the dream. They get those jobs, work their way through the institutions, and gradually discover how resistant these organizations can be to real change. They stay in them—they still have to pay the rent—but look back on their days engaged in less structured organizing longingly. This all likely sounds abstract to you, but there is a clear and observable difference in what professional organizers can do compared to their unencumbered volunteer counterparts who don't need a thumbs-up from the boss or to fill out a form.

I have a friend who used to lead one of these nonprofits. She's a radical with impeccable political bona fides. She led the organization well and was respected by others in her field. She spent a majority of her time gladhanding donors, managing the expectations of her board, and engaged in endless administrative tasks that were required to maintain the organization's tax status and to keep the lights on. Eventually, she left for another position, a step down in terms of status but a return to more direct, on-the-ground organizing work. I'm arguing here that there's an activist "brain drain" thanks to nonprofits, that a lot of dedicated and bright organizers end up moving paper around for these groups when they were previously involved in actions that were far more directly related to the lives of people in need. I'm also arguing that, as these nonprofit workers move up in the organizational hierarchy, earning fancier titles and better pay, they pull further and further away from the vital causes that once inspired them. It's the nature of nonprofits to take radicals and make them bureaucrats.

In the summer of 2020, when billions of dollars were unexpectedly earmarked for social justice, many progressive organizations were suddenly hiring, particularly seeking young activists of color. It wasn't unusual for someone to be outside in the streets organizing one week and sitting in a cubicle helping one of those organizations the next. I wondered at the time, looking out at the undeniable energy of the protests, if this was a step forward or a step back. The street protests were messy, disorganized, and working toward vague goals; the nonprofits are conservative no matter their charter, obsess over fundraising, and focus first on perpetuating their own existence. It is still not clear to me which is worse.

Perhaps it's not novel to say that too much structure and too much chaos are the Scylla and Charybdis of leftist action. People have lamented the difficulty in balancing the freedom and inspiration of unstructured activism with the accountability and planning of institutions for decades. And certainly, most of the problems I have discussed are not unique to the nonprofit space. But this vexing condition is particularly acute here.

I will leave you with one last concern about nonprofits: for many, they may provide a cheap sense of absolution. The experience of looking out at your world and your society and feeling a sense of unease and dissatisfaction with the way things are is the most basic stuff of politics—the sensation that something must be done. Without it there would be no organizers, no protests, no movement. The challenge for twenty-first-century agents of change is to cultivate and harness this internal demand for a better world. In 2020, injustice became so obvious and acute that we suddenly enjoyed a surplus of this essential resource. Many marched; many hung signs; some joined progressive organizations. And many, very many, wrote checks. Writing a check is better than nothing. But without a clear strategic approach to politics, carefully developed and expressed demands, and the capacity to organize intelligently, all the money in the world won't lead to justice. When George Floyd was murdered in the street in Minneapolis in 2020, countless Americans suddenly found themselves possessed of the demand for change. My worry is that for too many of them, that feeling was satiated by donating to a nonprofit organization. Today, when the fire of 2020 has largely died down, I fear that this temptation will prove even more alluring, donating money to assuage one's guilt. To build a new future, we need engaged voters, passionate organizers, skillful communicators, and eloquent advocates. Cutting a check is nice. But nice is all it is.

Nonprofits have a key role to play in building a more progressive future; they're needed to create the order necessary to achieve change. But I also think that the problems are abundant enough that we as a community of left organizers need to take a hard look at these institutions and their actual influence on our movements. That they function as a massive drain on tax revenues should offend our dedication to a vibrant social safety net; that they steer radical people into positions defined by bureaucratic tedium should worry us about the vibrance and sustainability of our movements. As with so much else in left politics, nonprofits prove to us again that the road to hell is paved with good intentions.

5

#MEMETOO

Few political movements in recent memory have packed quite so much emotional punch, or generated as much press, as #MeToo.

Though the term "#MeToo" was first coined in 2006, it gained widespread use as a result of allegations against the movie producer (and now convicted sex criminal) Harvey Weinstein. The rise of #MeToo was an organic reaction to decades of sexual misconduct in the entertainment industry, and later, in other fields. Hundreds of prominent men were named and shamed for engaging in unwanted sexual conduct, with many careers effectively ending as a result. The movement began in Hollywood but soon spread out to almost any field you can name, as more and more people—mostly but not exclusively women—came forward with their stories. The specific target of #MeToo was always clear: men who commit acts of sexual aggression, particularly in the workplace. The goal too had an admirable degree of clarity: no more sexual misconduct. To achieve this, the unofficial distributed network that made up #MeToo amplified accusations, defended the women who made them, and pushed for consequences. While many critics emerged to argue that

#MeToo was provoking a rush to judgment, few political movements have captured such a sense of electricity and momentum. In 2017 and for years afterward, it seemed clear that #MeToo was a powerful force for accountability. In addition to Weinstein, actor Kevin Spacey, singer R. Kelly, and comedian Bill Cosby all faced serious legal repercussions for their history of alleged misdeeds, to go along with dozens or hundreds who saw their careers take a major blow from allegations. (No verdict has been reached against Spacey as of this date.) #MeToo was a force, and many, many men feared it.

And yet many will now tell you that #MeToo has run out of steam. The unprecedented sense of emotional propulsion that attended the movement has faded. More and more of the accused seem to survive allegations that would have once ended careers. The allegations that are made receive less press. The accused are no longer assumed of being guilty, at least not to the same degree. The energy and passion that attended the movement seem to have faded. In October 2022, the *New York Times* summed up these feelings in an article titled "After #MeToo Reckoning, a Fear Hollywood Is Regressing." "Certainly," the article reads, "much of the fervor is gone."

Perhaps the best specific example of this can be seen in the much-sensationalized defamation trial that Johnny Depp won against his ex-wife, Amber Heard, in response to accusations of abuse Heard had made against Depp. After separating from Depp, Heard had written an essay in the *Washington Post* that, while it did not name Depp specifically, made it clear that Heard was alleging abuse on the part of Depp. Depp, in turn, lost work in Hollywood, with some claiming that his career was over. While Depp was accused of domestic violence rather than sexual misconduct, the trial was still seen as a referendum on the status of #MeToo in 2022. The case received enormous media attention, with many in the public picking sides and rooting for their preferred outcome.

In the end, defying much of the pretrial analysis, the jury decided in Depp's favor, finding that Heard had defamed him. (The jury also found that Depp's lawyer had defamed Heard.) Depp was awarded millions in damages and eventually settled with Heard.

The case was represented, by people across the political spectrum, as a bellwether. What signaled a new era was not merely that Depp won his case and was awarded a decision in the millions of dollars but rather that there was a large pro-Depp movement online, particularly among young women on the social media video app TikTok. The pro-Depp sentiment went viral, and the age and gender makeup of those who championed it cut directly against assumptions about who would most likely support #MeToo. There was a time when it would have been unthinkable for hashtags in support of accused abusers to trend on Twitter, but pro-Depp topics trended on a daily basis during the trial. The culture war was no longer being decisively won. As a *Vox* article stated in response to the Depp trial, "The long-awaited and much-dreaded backlash to the Me Too movement is here."

Why? Why has a movement that was once both beloved and feared in equal measure come to seem somewhat defanged? There have been a number of specific setbacks that have slowed the #MeToo movement, and the level of absolute fervor in 2017 and 2018 was never going to be sustained. But I think #MeToo has suffered because of its profoundly twenty-first-century nature of the movement—because #MeToo has always been, before and above everything else, a meme. #MeToo has had some profound real-world consequences, salutary ones, but the move-ment itself has always lived online. And I believe that this is the ultimate vulnerability of #MeToo: It is the nature of memes to rise and fall. Memes become popular, they begin to saturate online culture, and then they recede. That is the way of online culture, and that is the weakness of online politics.

It wasn't supposed to be this way. Early on, some in the #MeToo world seemed to recognize that the movement needed to move offline, for the torch to be carried by in-real-life organizations. The most prominent of these organizations was Time's Up, a much-ballyhooed, well-financed operation that was founded by some of the most powerful women in Hollywood. Time's Up was intended to be the organizational arm of #MeToo, a nonprofit that could rake in donation dollars and then use that money to raise awareness, work with studios to ensure gender equality on set, and perhaps file lawsuits or otherwise provide support for women who alleged workplace sexual misconduct. When the organization launched in January 2018, it took out a full-page ad in the *New York Times* to circulate an open letter signed by celebrities like Natalie Portman and Reese Witherspoon. It spoke out to the world's victims of sexual harassment and assault and said, "We stand with you. We support you." Within two weeks of the publication of the open letter, the organization had raised $15 million. In the height of the #MeToo media narrative, an organization with the backing of some of the entertainment industry's most powerful women, a dedicated legal team, and deep pockets seemed formidable indeed.

Alas.

Since that original rush of success, Time's Up has come undone, and in a cruelly ironic way. An October 2022 report in the *Hollywood Reporter* detailed Time's Up's "implosion," describing it as "a leaderless ghost organization." The article described rampant infighting and considerable turmoil over a variety of issues, but nothing damaged Time's Up more than the Andrew Cuomo affair. Cuomo, who ruled with unusual power as the governor of New York and was at one point seen as perhaps the future of the Democratic Party, was accused by multiple women who worked alongside him of sexual misconduct, including verbal innuendos and inappropriate touching. Cuomo repeatedly denied wrongdoing and for months resisted calls for his resignation, but over time his position became untenable. In 2021, he gave up his office. In the fallout of this scandal, it emerged that some of the top leadership at Time's Up had advised Cuomo on how to handle the public relations of those accusations. In other words, a vehicle for amplifying accusations of sexual misconduct had served to help minimize such accusations. The optics could hardly be worse for an organization dedicated to supporting women who were alleging sexually inappropriate behavior. Several members of the board resigned in response, and the organization became, from my perspective, rudderless and dysfunctional. Emails to Time's Up by the *Hollywood Reporter* were met with formulaic responses that the nonprofit was undergoing "an organizational rebuild"; as I was finishing the manuscript for this book in January 2023, it was announced that Time's Up was closing its doors.

In a certain sense, the decline of one particular organization dedicated to fighting workplace sexual misconduct says little about the health of the broader movement. And yet the disintegration of the most prominent formal vehicle for advancing #MeToo spoke to a deeper structural problem with that movement. The deferential treatment of Cuomo, a powerful Democrat, helps underline the fundamental problem with using trial by public relations as your basic mechanism for achieving justice. Cuomo was forced from office thanks to public pressure, and the case against him seems fairly strong, so you could see his resignation as a just outcome. But the fact that he was sheltered at the heights of the Time's Up organization, and why—it's impossible to imagine a Republican politician receiving similar support—speaks to the sense that the consequences meted out by #MeToo have always been fickle. Whether one becomes a target of the movement's ire has often been bound up in preexisting questions of influence and power. The core of the problem with #MeToo, and with all attempts to dispense justice online, is inconsistency. The experience of a specific, powerful politician may be sui generis, but the lack of consistency from case to case is all too common. The jerry-rigged nature of trial by internet makes such inconsistency inevitable. Yes, Weinstein was taken down, but his crimes were so numerous, so utterly constant throughout his career, that his trial felt less like a victory and more like a memorial to his victims. The victories have a way of underlining the continuing systemic problems.

The subhead of a *Washington Post* piece about the consequences of #MeToo for various men accused of bad behavior captured this reality efficiently: "A few went to prison. Some have disappeared. But many are rebuilding their careers. And some were barely affected."

Consistency is core to most people's conception of justice; we believe that it can only be achieved if different people receive the same treatment for the same crimes. Of course, our legal system never achieves this goal, but the attempt at consistency and procedural uniformity animates the entire project of Western law. And even outside a formal legal framework, people want fairness and equity in judgment. I'm convinced that the inability of #MeToo to attain such consistency has been a key part of its declining salience. Observers of #MeToo can look at the experiences of different men who have been accused, note the differences in how they have been affected by the accusations, and fairly question whether justice can be achieved through those means. If some men essentially have their careers erased by allegations, while similarly accused men avoid real consequence, public confidence in the movement will naturally be reduced.

Take Neil deGrasse Tyson, the famous scientist and media personality who has been something like the public face of astrophysics for many years. Tyson is the director of the Hayden Planetarium at the Museum of Natural History in New York City, holds myriad positions in various organizations and universities, has a successful podcast, and is involved in several television shows. This enviable professional success was seemingly threatened in late 2018, when he was accused of sexual misconduct by four different women. These allegations ranged from inappropriate comments to drugging and raping a fellow graduate student. Tyson disputed that he had ever committed sexual misconduct, and no criminal charges were ever brought. Still, these were the kinds of allegations that we had come to see as existentially damning, in a #MeToo world, but while the accusations were amplified for a news cycle and several investigations by his employers were launched, Tyson appears to have suffered no major repercussions. The investigations concluded without consequence, and he maintained his various cushy gigs. More, his public persona as an affable science communicator barely seems to have been affected; he's often sought out for participation in various projects or comments on science stories, without any indication that he was accused at all. (It is, however, true that he has not added to his collection of twenty honorary degrees since the allegations.)

I have no special knowledge of the allegations against Tyson, and I have no interest in trying to litigate whether the accusations are true. What I am interested in here is the way he escaped serious repercussions from the kinds of allegations that had quickly destroyed other men. And I am interested in this question specifically because such inconsistency undermines the faith of the general public in a social movement, making it more difficult for that movement to make positive change. "Some of the most galvanizing early #MeToo cases suggested that a thorough and eternal discrediting would be the fate of every accused man," the *Washington Post* piece put it, "but outside of a bad news cycle, others haven't really been affected at all." I could name others who have been accused with little consequence, such as the actor Morgan Freeman (accused by eight women), progressive politician Keith Ellison, or entertainment personality Ryan Seacrest. (Seacrest and Ellison vehemently denied any allegations; Freeman also denied that he had assaulted anyone or created a hostile work environment, but apologized for anyone he may have upset.) If nothing else, this lack of uniformity in consequence gives everyone accused of sexual misconduct a valid criticism of the movement.

But the deeper problem with #MeToo, I think, was that its strength was also its weakness: its power was derived from the news cycle. When allegations and their consequences dominated the media conversation, the glare of public opprobrium could force a reaction. Occasionally, attorneys general or the police were motivated to bring charges against the accused; more often, private actors could suspend or fire people, cancel future projects with them, or otherwise attack them professionally. And with several major figures, like Kevin Spacey, essentially having their careers ended by such negative publicity, the tactic seemed to work. For several years #MeToo hummed along, with more and more men receiving public accusations and negative publicity, although questions of fairness always followed. In 2018, it wasn't hard to believe that the movement would go on changing the world perpetually.

The trouble with utilizing public attention and the news cycle, though, is that the public and the media are both fickle. The nature of public attention is to change its focus over time; the news cycle is a cycle because it changes over time. And a phenomenon as deeply driven by emotion as #MeToo could never have maintained that same sense of visceral importance. The heady early days of palpable public anger and seemingly endless new accusations could never be perfectly preserved over time. In the title of this chapter I refer to the movement as #MemeToo, as the movement spread in just the same way that a meme travels on the internet. The expression of an idea grabs the attention of a few, they broadcast it to their online networks, more and more people do the same, and suddenly the idea becomes inescapable. The trouble is that memes go stale; that is their nature. Once a saturation point is reached, fatigue sets in, and the energy that powered the meme is dissipated. The public fixation on a given meme can be intense, but is always brief. And sadly, it appears that over time, it became harder and harder for the collective consciousness to remain as shocked and disgusted by sexual misconduct allegations as it once had been. This is of course not a normative claim I'm making; I'm not suggesting that the public *should* gradually lose interest in sexual misconduct, gradually growing numb to the parade of awful behavior and traumatized victims. I am suggesting that, as lamentable as it may be, the public *did* grow numb to #MeToo. And this is far from unique in social movements; the horror of George Floyd's murder remains powerful, but the intensity of the immediate period following his murder could never be sustained.

Perhaps some of #MeToo's champions contributed to this gradual loss of shock and impulse for change. Inevitably, some of the allegations were less clear-cut than those against Weinstein, who was accused of all manner of unwanted sexual behavior by dozens of women, and for whom there was documented evidence of years of abuse. Other allegations were less certain. The more examples of gray area and conflicting stories that emerged, the less clarity and force the movement seemed to have. The most infamous example of this dynamic lay in allegations against the actor and comic Aziz Ansari. In 2018, in a small (and now defunct) publication called Babe.net, a woman who had spent a night with Ansari detailed his behavior. Ansari was accused of being sexually pushy and too forward, putting the accuser in an awkward position that made her, in her words, uneasy. But Ansari was expressly, and notably, not accused of nonconsensual sexual behavior of the kind that so many others had been. This did not prevent a media firestorm, as the Ansari story dominated social media for days and produced an immense amount of response pieces. Ansari published a statement insisting that everything that happened was completely consensual, which the initial allegations did not dispute; he did, however, express regret over what had happened. What was unusual in the brief history of #MeToo was the number of people who defended Ansari or, at least, argued that he did not deserve to be placed in the same category as Weinstein, Spacey, or many others. For example, the feminist writer Jill Filipovic, who has been a vocal champion of #MeToo, argued that the Ansari story should not have been run and did a disservice to the broader movement.

Again, I do not write this to suggest that the existence of disagreements about who is or is not guilty of sexual misconduct *should* result in less faith in the broader movement. I don't suggest that the Ansari situation specifically undermines the broader #MeToo movement. What I am suggesting is that, as we inevitably witnessed cases where the reality was contested and the justice of the attempted cancellation was controversial, the energy and clarity of the movement was bound to dissipate. And dissipate it has.

It's important not to be overly critical. The impulse behind #MeToo has always been noble, and the effort to fight sexual misconduct in Hollywood and elsewhere is driven by real need. Some accused of genuinely bad acts, such as Weinstein, the singer R. Kelly, and the actor Danny Masterson have faced real legal consequences, and the removal of people like them from the industry will at least contribute to community safety. (Masterson's first trial for sexual assault ended in a mistrial, and he denies all wrongdoing.) The world remains filled with sexually predatory men, and if #MeToo was not always the perfect instrument for dealing with that problem, none had ever had such a powerful effect before. I also recognize that there was no clear way that things could have gone differently, no obvious better path. Yes, #MeToo suffered for being a meme, but you and I know it exists because of its memetic power; there would be nothing for me to write about in this chapter had #MeToo not become a meme. It's tempting to say that things would have been different had Time's Up lived up to the intentions of its founders, but this very book argues that the nonprofits that make up the institutions of progressivism are bound to fall short of their missions. It appears to be a nasty catch-22—institutionalizing an organic movement leaves it subject to institutional capture, the dilution of effort into managerialism and bureaucracy; failing to institutionalize inhibits clear messages and ensures that there is little individual accountability for missteps or failure to achieve change. If nothing else, perhaps we can say that #MeToo would have benefited from more message discipline and clarity of targets. This would be hard to achieve, given that the movement has always been decentralized and leaderless. But perhaps there's another world where #MeToo would have remained more focused and thus more powerful.

Of course #MeToo is not dead, and it's possible that another prominent accusation, against a particularly powerful or beloved figure, could galvanize the movement back to its previous stature. #MeToo may rise again. More depressingly, you can imagine a future where the ambitious and powerful routinely misuse #MeToo for their own purposes. You might consider the case of Jeff Zucker, the former executive vice president and chief marketing officer of CNN, who was forced to resign after it was revealed that he had engaged in a consensual relationship with a coworker. It's been alleged that this was less a matter of enforcing proper workplace conduct and more the fallout of a power struggle within the corporate structure. I recognize that workplace leaders dating subordinates is a fraught business, but it's possible that Zucker's ouster was less about such concerns and more about corporate brinksmanship. There's no way to be sure if this theory of Zucker's ouster is true, but the fact remains that movements as influential as #MeToo become attractive opportunities for misuse. Zucker, for his part, acknowledged the affair and apologized for failing to disclose it. It's no insult to #MeToo to suggest that the movement might be misused in the way I'm suggesting. But that which we empower, we ensure will be exploited.

What are the lessons for the broader progressive project? The simplest and most powerful is simply this: there is no such thing as an online social movement. Political projects that extend no further than a web browser will always be subject to faddishness and burnout. The internet is fickle; it frequently amounts to a record of the day-to-day whims of bored people. Of course the tools of online connectivity can be used to satisfy political ends, if they are deployed strategically—informing people about issues, urging them to get out the vote. But the internet cannot be the prime mover of political change. The typical narrative of success stories from internet-enabled politics, like the Arab Spring (which now looks much less like a success than it once did), tends to reductively ascribe change to social media. But preexisting socioeconomic conditions laid the groundwork for the internet-enabled communication that drove the Arab Spring protests, and in turn, protestors left the internet and took to the streets. #MeToo sparked protests and prompted congressional inquiries, among other in-real-life consequences. But the actual day-to-day prosecution of the movement remains online. This was not so much a choice by any party as a function of the movement's most basic processes. And the fundamental inconsistency and lack of specific personal responsibility that attends online social movements has harmed the fight against sexual misconduct.

Which gets to another great difficulty with #MeToo: it has both pursued numerous targets (in the form of the individual bad men who it has attempted to take down) and yet lacked a clear target in terms of a specific policy goal. An unusual element of #MeToo was that much of the bad behavior it aimed to stamp out was already actively illegal or, at least, against corporate policies and institutional mandates. Harvey Weinstein is in jail because his bad behaviors were against the law. Many less-notable bad men lost their jobs in the #MeToo wave because their sexual misconduct violated their corporate sexual harassment policies.

There are certainly proposed changes to law and policy that some involved with #MeToo have advanced, but fundamentally the demand has been that existing laws be enforced. This is part of why #MeToo has been advanced with such righteous rage—the laws were already on the books, and yet the people tasked with enforcing them were failing women. But that meant that no clear central policy demand ever emerged as the core organizing principle for the movement; there was no great #MeToo Act of 2019. And so #MeToo becomes a kind of Whac-A-Mole, effectively knocking down some bad actors only to see more inevitably emerge. As I have argued so often throughout this text, a lack of clear and obvious legislative demands dooms social movements.

Which, I know, sounds harsh toward #MeToo, a fundamentally righteous movement that makes a demand that could hardly be simpler, more necessary, or more powerful: Stop preying on women. Stop committing sexual misconduct. Allow everyone to feel safe in the workplace, and everywhere else. These are all important goals. And, as you'd expect, there are a lot of people who are still committed to #MeToo and will continue to vocally advocate for consequences for men who are guilty of sexual offenses. That's as it should be. I'm not writing this to advocate for the end of #MeToo. I am writing to argue that a certain amount of exhaustion with the project was inevitable, as from the beginning it was inextricable from the meme culture that powered and organized it. All movements have limitations. This one presents an opportunity to better understand the appropriate use of digital tools.

What's unusual about #MeToo in political history, but increasingly the case in the broader contemporary progressive movement, is that the political action *is* an expression. That is to say, in political organizing our expressions (our slogans, our literature, our outreach) are tools to achieve a particular end. Generally speaking, this means rallying support for a given cause or candidate, trying to win hearts and minds either for political ends (such as getting a candidate elected or a ballot referendum passed) or to provoke some direct action (such as convincing workers to strike). In this traditional form of political engagement, the expressions always serve the movement and provoke future action.

In today's activist culture, expressions are often the ends themselves. Canceling, or making critiques or accusations with the intent of provoking widespread personal and professional shunning, is an example of where the political action stops at the level of expression. "MeTooing" proved to be perhaps the most powerful version of canceling, and individual targets have had their public personae effectively vaporized. The question is, what happens next? If the accusation works, then an abuser is potentially removed from a position of power. But stamping out sexual misconduct has a treadmill quality to it; there's always another target coming. A more traditional political movement might have its sights set on a particular piece of transformative legislation that could address a systemic problem.

To be fair to those who have taken part in the movement, #MeToo activists have always wanted structural change. Organizations like Time's Up were meant to help facilitate such change, and the organization, in fact, maintained a long list of demands, centering around safety, equity, and power. In addition to the most obvious demand "that every person is free from sexual harassment, assault, retaliation, and other forms of discrimination on the job," the demands also included equity and power for women in the workplace. As far as nonprofit platform-speak goes, the Time's Up demands were inoffensive. The trouble is, first, despite the voluminous amount of text on the website, there was still a lack of partic-ularly tangible goals, owing in part to the previously discussed problem that much of ending sexual misconduct amounts to enforcing rules rather than legislating new ones. And more, there appears to have been far more organic desire to participate by naming and shaming than through steadily building power and creating change. For many supporters of

#MeToo, that support seems to end at their laptop screen—which is not an unusual circumstance in the twenty-first century.

This is part of the fundamental trouble with meme politics: memes are powered by novelty and the rush of shared attention. The question for political movements that spread like memes is, what happens when the rush is over and the hard work begins? We live in an era where it is possible to easily provoke politicized outrage, but we have few recent success stories when it comes to maintaining that initial momentum. As we drifted from the heady days of 2020 and the inciting incidents of much of the progressive outrage that defined it, structures were not built that could ensure that work continue without the heat of mass attention. In one sense, #MeToo is better equipped to survive than any other recent political program—anyone, at any time, can use the power of media (social or traditional) to make an accusation, and despite whatever stalled momentum the movement faces, sometimes the allegations stick. But from another perspective, #MeToo is hamstrung, as the online world is both the site of its practice and the source of its power. The difficulty of translating the energy and anger of the online world to the offline world can't be underestimated, and the lack of clear material goals, which haunts so many left movements, hangs heavy here. Perhaps #MeToo will simply endure as a perpetual sense of greater accountability for sexual misconduct, picking off a target here or there. If so, that sounds like a kind of victory. But it's fair to wonder if this has all been a missed opportunity to accomplish more.

What left organizers can perhaps learn from #MeToo is how difficult it can be for a movement to survive when it spreads like a meme.

6

MEET THE GOODIES:
WHY ARE LIBERALS THE
WAY THEY ARE?

Consider the liberal.

Or perhaps I should say, consider the liberal once again. Reconsider the liberal, if you will. Few groups have been analyzed more often than the liberal, the American progressive, the center-left Democrat. They are a group of unique sociological interest, in part because most people who perform sociology hail from that tribe themselves. The word itself is notoriously contested; the boundaries of the category are certainly squishy, and the term is seemingly used as a pejorative more often than in self-identification. Some libertarians and conservatives demand that they are "classical liberals," following in the lineage of John Locke and Adam Smith, but many of their beliefs are the opposite of what we mean when we say "liberal" now. In the Clinton '90s, many Democrats fled from the label, seeing it as a vestige of the left-wing excesses of the 1960s and '70s. In the mid-2010s, the insults began to pile up from the opposite direction as a new generation of strident socialists derided their more centrist peers. Everyone recognizes that liberals are an influential group in American politics, but few seem willing to carry the label. And yet "liberal" remains a word of potent explanatory power, contested though it may be. I have spent much of this book discussing the activist left, but, in the long term, the numerically far larger group of American liberals will do more to shape the future.

For my purposes here, I'll use "liberal" to describe those left-leaning Americans who defend capitalism as long as it operates under regulatory constraints and with appropriate redistributive mechanisms. They may be routinely critical of Democrats, but vote for them just as routinely and disdain third parties. They concede that our meritocracy is imperfect and frequently produces unjust results, but defend the meritocratic ideal. They're reliably forward-looking in regard to social norms, forever chasing the identity vanguard, but tend to practice traditional family formation themselves. They believe broadly in economic justice and will typically include higher taxes for the wealthy in that concept but become reliably vague when it comes to how much higher taxes should be and who qualifies as "wealthy." They tend to be arch institutionalists, favoring expert opinion and remaining doggedly invested in establishment news media, frequently deferring to the wisdom of the CDC, the Democratic Party's power structure, and MSNBC. They are left-of-center but right-of-left. They are the liberals.

Conservatives, of course, have been examining the liberal mind for as long as movement conservatism has existed. But analysis from the left-of-center provides us with a huge amount of material as well; liberals are a group that has been subject to constant anthropological examination. And as much as they are mocked, derided, and parodied, the successful liberal of the 2020s remains an aspirational figure.

The Democratic Party is the left-leaning American party, and most left-leaning Americans vote Democrat. But it's important to say that when

I speak about liberals, I'm not talking about the average Democrat. In public polling, a majority of Democrats do not self-identify as liberals. A 2022 Gallup poll found that 38 percent of registered Democrats identified as moderates, with another 12 percent identifying as conservative. This means that while a plurality of Democrats identifies as liberal, just as many do not. You may contrast this with the Republican Party, where fully 74 percent of registered voters identify as conservative. This, as much as anything, explains the tendency of the Democrats to be incrementalist and cautious where Republicans are bold and inflammatory. These tendencies, as much as they inflame liberal Democrats, are a reflection of the priorities of the base of the respective parties. Unfortunately, from my perspective, given my leftist politics.

Liberals angry about the lack of bold progressive leadership from Democrats might point to affluent white voters as the source of their problems, but the polling does not bear this out. A 2020 Pew poll, in keeping with decades-long trends, found that only 29 percent of Black Democrats self-identified as liberal, while 55 percent of white Democrats did. Despite the constant radical invocation of people of color as a kind of political talisman, the left wing of the Democratic Party is overwhelmingly white. "Since 2000," read the Pew research paper, "the share of Black Democrats who describe their political views as liberal has changed little, while liberal identification among white Democrats has nearly doubled." And, while Gallup's polling shows that in the country writ large there are no obvious income effects on who identifies as liberal, liberal identification is vastly more common among educated people than those without educational credentials, with 36 percent of those with postgraduate degrees in America identifying as liberal, whereas only 19 percent of those with no college do so. The median Democrat leans left less dramatically than the median Republican leans right, and this is because of less-educated voters and voters of color.

When I talk about liberals, I won't mean the median Democrat but instead the approximately 15 percent of the party that self-identifies as "very liberal." It's from this slice of the American electorate that our left-of-center writers, journalists, pundits, and analysts are overwhelmingly drawn. Including me—while I wouldn't happily accept the label "liberal" myself, in polling where the furthest-left group is called "very liberal," that's where I belong. It's that 15 percent that generates the vast share of any conversation about what's best for our country and the Democratic Party politically, and it's the distance between that group's political values and the median voter that generates so much political angst. To consider what makes vocal liberals what they are, we need to do a little sociology.

A TAXONOMY OF THE CONTEMPORARY AMERICAN LIBERAL

Perhaps a good place to start is a text from what I would consider the early days of what constitutes contemporary liberalism. David Brooks, the longtime *New York Times* columnist and many people's platonic ideal of a centrist, wrote a turn-of-the-millennium-era book titled *Bobos in Paradise*. ("Turn of the millennium," as in published on January 1, 2000.) The book meticulously chronicles the habits of the titular "bobos"—the bohemian bourgeois—who yearn to accumulate wealth like their fore-fathers, but insist on doing so in a more enlightened style. The bobo wants a nice house and expensive car, but they also want to save the planet and live a kind of subtle zen critique of the system. Though far from a majority in numbers, bobos are the intellectual foot soldiers of the modern Democratic Party. Educated and upwardly mobile, if not already affluent, the bohemian bourgeois donate to the nonprofits that set the policy agenda, volunteer for the campaigns that produce the leaders, and chew the ears of the politicians of their party. They write the editorials that appear in the newspapers and do more than their fair share of arguing and complaining in the public sphere.

Core to this class of people is the strange tension between their beliefs in the predominance of structural factors and systems when speaking about political issues and their tendency toward delayed gratification in their own lives. One element of modern liberalism that Brooks gets very right is the modern liberal's attachment to discipline and self-improvement. Brooks describes a species of person who has been raised to see self-denial and hard work as essential, even as they espouse a politics that places less emphasis on personal responsibility and more on social. "They turn nature into an achievement course," wrote Brooks, "a series of ordeals and obstacles they can conquer." The liberal urbanite who puts signs in their window to identify with the latest progressive cause is not someone who wants to live off the government generosity that they advocate for but someone who wants to feel that their station is deserved by dint of their willingness to work and sacrifice. This striving spirit is part of why liberals are so influential, and also underlies one of many tensions within the contemporary liberal project.

I remember meeting a friend for lunch here in my liberal enclave in Brooklyn. He came toddler in tow, and his son squirmed and made little-kid noises and whimpered repeatedly. Eventually, his son made clear that he wanted one of the yogurt parfaits in the bistro's glass case. (In the kid's defense, they did look delicious.) The trouble, from the father's perspective, was that the parfait was no doubt "just loaded with sugar." He asked his son in somber tones, "Are you sure you're making a healthy choice?" The kid whimpered a bit more but quickly took the hint; he ended up with carrot sticks and hummus instead. Clearly the son really didn't have much of a choice at all, in any meaningful sense. I don't think he would have gotten that parfait no matter how hard he held out. But it was clearly important to the father that his son *believe* he had a choice and that he make the right one. That emphasis on choice, on the agency of the child and the potential consequence of choosing, is on constant display in liberal parenting in the twenty-first century. In the six-plus years I lived in Brooklyn, I regularly saw the "making a healthy choice" scene. It fits in perfectly with Brooks's vision of the bobo—to be a good progressive, one must practice a certain kind of self-denial, self-denial that will tend over time to lead to greater fiscal security and social status.

Affluent white liberals raise their offspring to (choose to) do their homework before they play, to (choose to) be active and eat healthy foods, to (choose to) devote their undivided attention and effort to their extracurricular activities like pottery or martial arts; to (choose to) stick with their violin practice rather than to play video games; to (choose to) sit and learn dutifully during their myriad educational clubs. They are taught to see life as a series of choices that will ultimately determine their opportunities and financial security in life.

In other words, liberals tend to exemplify in their own lives and inculcate in the minds of their children an *internal locus of control*. Locus of control, according to *Psychology Today*, refers to "an individual's belief system regarding the causes of his or her experiences and the factors to which that person attributes success or failure." It's a reflexive understanding of why one's life happens the way it happens. Those with an internal locus of control tend to believe that their own choices and behaviors play a determinative role in their lives, while those with an external locus of control tend to assume that their lives are determined largely by outside forces. Contemporary liberals, like the bobos before them, act like they can determine the course of their own lives through smart choices and through the practice of personal discipline, their secular sacrament.

The tension here is obvious. The selfsame helicopter parents who insist that their children delay gratification and make smart, forward-thinking choices evince political opinions that minimize the importance of those same decisions. After all, it's liberals who fixate relentlessly on privilege, defined as *unearned* (and uncontrollable) advantage that accrues to some by dint of an identity category. It's liberals who—accurately and humanely, in my view—look at the working poor and the homeless and see the hand of forces they can't control. It's liberals who reject the conservative ethos of the self-made man, liberals who talk about structural forces that dictate winners and losers. And, at times, they talk and act in a way consistent with belief in those forces.

Appropriately contextualized, belief in external locus of control is all for the good. The trouble is not the political belief that all of us are buffeted by the hands of fate and that we should thus form a society in which we make allowances for those who labor under the burdens of structural oppression and bad luck. The trouble is that, especially in the era of social media where all stray thoughts are subject to validation by others, some have mistaken this political stance for an endorsement of the view that they are permanent victims who can do nothing to control their own lives. In a brilliant 2022 essay called "Failure to Cope 'Under Capitalism,'" the socialist writer Clare Coffey diagnosed the contemporary left obsession with seeing life as a series of obstacles beyond one's control—and deciding therefore not to try. Coffey wrote:

> There is a strain of discourse that insists an inability to cope in one's day-to-day life is in almost all cases a political problem, or even the primary political problem. . . . Sometimes it's an elaborate hypothetical in which asking a disabled person to make alternate arrangements and forgo ordering Instacart groceries for one day of a strike is tantamount to a genocidal program. Sometimes it's a prompt tweet inviting you into a post-revolutionary fantasy world where, instead of collecting municipal garbage, you will be "doing art.". . . Somehow, being born into a historical moment when moderate clerical abilities can lead

to impressive status and resource acquisition is still to be crippled by fate, NPCs, or Soros agents.

What binds these pleas together is an application of "the personal is political" so expanded in scope that, for a certain kind of person, personal problems, anxieties, and dissatisfactions are illegible or illegitimate unless described as political problems.

Coffey, herself on the left, is not making this complaint from a conservative perspective. Her point is not to blame the poor for their poverty or to excuse capitalism for producing inequality and alienation. Her point is that, when let loose from any coherent political ideology, ascribing every negative element of human life to political forces you can't control leaves you helpless. Of course our lives are influenced by powerful external systems. But life compels us to work within them, and we can do better or worse at that task. The trick, then, is to teach people not only to recognize that poverty and hardship are not simplistically the product of an individual's choices but also to understand that no political victory will suddenly remove all the problems of life. We can't control everything with our choices; we must still make choices, and try to make the better ones, nevertheless. We live our lives in that contradiction.

As a Marxist, I see a great deal to agree with in the concept of external locus of control; Marxists, after all, believe that the progress of history is drawn by great structural forces, not the efforts of individuals. The proletariat are not in that station because of a lack of work ethic but because of vast economic systems that existed before they were born and will exist after they're dead. But there's a profound difference between the explicit politics of justifying rigorous government redistributive programs and the sense that one's life is simply and entirely out of one's hands, a self-exonerating impulse to blame the system for everything. And as I've suggested, a core tension among many liberal commentators is the ability to maintain this avowed belief in external locus of control while working like busy little meritocrats in their personal and professional lives.

There's a quality of ritual to the way that liberal success stories transition so easily (and so reliably) from the dogged pursuit of meritocratic success to disdaining that very system once they have comfortably secured their position within it. During their adolescence they sweat—day and night—to get into the right college, take advantage of an unfathomable amount of classes and clubs and opportunities once there, then land jobs that will put them on the path to enviable upwardly mobile American lives—at which point they promptly discover disdain for the very system that they were so recently dedicated to. I doubt any individual of these programs and practices does a great deal to move the needle, but the aggregate influence of that many "good choices" on life outcomes may help explain intergenerational success.

In the introduction to the 2011 edition of his book *The Paradise Suite: Bobos in Paradise and* On Paradise Drive, Brooks looked back and found that the bobos and their spiritual children were still possessed of an ethos of self-denial and, increasingly, a lack of comfort with their own financial comfort. "It is still true that they are ambivalent about their success," wrote Brooks, "and they clothe their affluence in moral, organic, and environmental drapery." The young father fretting over his son's healthy choices was, in part, simply an artifact of his desire for his child to live a healthy life. But it was also an emblem of the affluent progressive's desire to live without guilt, to justify their comfortable station in life.

A conservative who believes that people usually get what they deserve and that success is determined by hard work can simply luxuriate without guilt in any good fortune. But liberals are bent on seeing their own affluent status in contrast with the financial struggles of those they see, correctly, as suffering due at least in part to structural factors beyond their control. Perversely, this sense of ambient guilt over success seems to compel them to double down on their self-conception as people of discipline who delay gratification and work hard for what they achieve, even in the shadow of their own understanding that the life outcomes of any given person lie significantly outside of their own control.

These are not just idle musings about the psychic pathologies of a certain species of affluent person. Locus of control stands as a major, frequently undiscussed element of contemporary politics. Summarizing a 2019 YouGov poll, John Hood of the *Carolina Journal* wrote:

> American conservatives are more likely than American progressives to express the internal-control view.
>
> Consider this statement: "My life is determined by my own actions." While 52 percent of respondents identified as very conservative agreed with this statement, only 33 percent of very liberal respondents agreed. Here's another one: "When I get what I want, it's usually because I worked hard for it." Support was 53 percent among the very conservative and 30 percent among the very liberal.
>
> Perhaps even more to the point: "I feel like what happens in my life is mostly determined by powerful people." Fully 61 percent of the very conservative respondents *disagreed* with this statement, while only 34 percent of the very liberal did.

This relationship between left political activity and attitude toward locus of control stretches far back: A 1976 study found that "for liberals, increases in expectancies of control by powerful others are positively associated with increases in activism, while for conservatives, there is a negative relationship." That is, believing that life outcomes were largely controllable by the individual inspired conservatives to more political activism, where the opposite belief inspired liberals.

THE MERITOCRATIC LIBERAL AND EDUCATION POLARIZATION

Yet, at least when it comes to education, those who set the tone in our political debates have opted for hard work and climbing the meritocratic ladder. An analysis by the National Association of Scholars found that "the overwhelming majority of the talking heads [that is, pundits and opinion makers] have college degrees; many of them have advanced degrees." That analysis was published in 2008, but there's little reason to think that college education has become less common among journalists and pundits in the years since. For example, a 2018 paper from the *Journal of Expertise* found that "almost half of the people who reach the pinnacle of the journalism profession attended an elite school. . . . This means top 1% people are overrepresented among the [*New York Times*] and [*Wall Street Journal*] mastheads by a factor of about 50." It's a fact widely understood within elite media, a field where I have enjoyed some success, that the profession is filled with a highly unrepresentative fringe of the most educated Americans. And getting into and through an elite college likely requires at least a degree of belief that one's own choices matter for one's life outcomes.

The political influence goes beyond mere shared experience. To understand where we are, it's essential to understand the rise of educational polarization as a defining factor—perhaps *the* defining factor for the more politically educated and engaged—in contemporary American political life. Education polarization refers to the way that the education level of a certain group predicts their ideological and political affiliation.

Some of the most important work on educational polarization has been conducted by Thomas Piketty, the French economist whose best-selling 2014 book, *Capital in the Twenty-First Century*, argued that wealth inequality rises over time due to the structural relationship between interest and growth. The book caused a sensation, a remarkable feat for a dry academic text of economic history. Following its success, Piketty aimed to explain why traditional divides in ideological coalitions appeared to be changing—why the left, so long the political vehicle of the common man, was becoming associated with elitism.

Piketty's 2018 article "Brahmin Left vs Merchant Right: Rising Inequality and the Changing Structure of Political Conflict" defined the general trend by saying that while in the 1950s and '60s left-wing political parties were largely supported by low-education, low-wage workers, the left "has gradually become associated with higher education voters, giving rise to a 'multiple-elite' party system in the 2000s–2010s: high-education elites now vote for the 'left,' while high-income/high-wealth elites still vote for the 'right' (though less and less so)." This dynamic can be seen in the most crude stereotypes about left and right: that the former are latte-swilling urbanites looking down their nose at "real America," while the latter are ignorant hicks, raging against the demise of white privilege and afraid of every imaginable change occurring to their country. Looking at data from post-election surveys in Britain, France, and the United States, Piketty's paper helped add more evidentiary weight to the popular conception of colleges as breeding grounds of left-wing thought. A piece by the right-leaning *Economist* summarized Piketty's argument by saying that the paper found that, in 1955, less-educated and lower-class voters chose left-leaning parties, while more educated and richer voters supported right-leaning ones. But today, while the economic dynamics still stand (lower class supporting left parties, upper class supporting right), by 2000 the higher-educated supported liberal parties more than lower-educated voters did. Since then, this dynamic has only intensified.

In September 2021, Nate Cohn of the *New York Times* summarized the effects of this polarization in writing "as they've grown in numbers, college graduates have instilled increasingly liberal cultural norms while gaining the power to nudge the Democratic Party to the left." As Cohn points out, this has major implications for who wins elections, far greater than in decades past. "Overall, 41 percent of people who cast ballots last year were four-year college graduates, according to census estimates. In contrast, just 5 percent of voters in 1952 were college graduates," wrote Cohn.

It's worth noting that engagement and turnout are also implicated in the education polarization question. Writing for the Mellon Foundation in 2019, Paula McAvoy, David Campbell, and Diana Hess report that greater investment in a liberal arts and social science education leads to "more participatory, engaged, and public-regarding citizenry," arguing that the rise in college education has helped raise voter turnout rates from their nadirs in the 1990s. So, college education seems to push people to the left, and also to inspire them to be more politically active once they're there. And, indeed, the voting and registration supplement to the 2020 Census found that turnout for high school graduates was 55.5 percent, while turnout for those with a bachelor's degree was 77.9 percent.

The bigger question is, why? What's caused this educational polarization?

It's tempting to believe that these are all selection effects—that is, that people already inclined to be socially liberal sort themselves into college, rather than college producing more socially liberal people causally. But the evidence suggests otherwise.

College does not merely marinate people in a particular political milieu but in social and cultural ones as well. College-educated people are also more likely to share trends in media consumption, fashion, and vocabulary. They're more likely to have read certain theories and foundational academic texts. And they're more likely to be exposed to broader cultural and demographic diversity; exposure to diversity, particularly earlier in life, is associated with left-wing views. The self-flattering explanation for a leftist like myself would be to point out that college increases knowledge of the world and, in doing so, brings people more into alignment with the correct way to think of that world. But this explanation is hopelessly confounded by one's definition of the truth. It's worth saying, however, that whether left-wing perspectives are correct or not, the association between years of education and ideology is not merely a matter of sorting. It may be tempting to conclude that people who are more left-wing are more likely to choose to go to college, so that the line of causation flows in the other direction. But recent high-quality research has found that the relationship is indeed causal: college makes people more left-wing. There's even reason to believe that the relationship between college and ideology is now more certain than the one between ideology and race.

Part of what's at play here may be the (partial and unequal) move to a more materially abundant society. In this telling, socially liberal beliefs are more prevalent in societies in which there are more people who live without fear of losing basic material security, and more prevalent among the more affluent within those societies. Reviewing the literature for *New York* magazine in 2022, Eric Levitz noted that "people who experience material security in youth tend to develop distinctive values and preferences from those who do not: if childhood teaches you to take your basic material needs for granted, you're more likely to develop culturally progressive values and post-material policy priorities." This is not entirely flattering to those who hold liberal values, as it makes such beliefs seem like luxury items. But it makes a great deal of sense: once people are able to assume that they will not be in a zero-sum battle with others for their most basic needs, they're able to open their minds to different kinds of difference, such as to racial minorities or immigrants—they no longer see the Other as competition for scarce resources. And this theory dovetails nicely with the fact that there is a college wage premium such that people with college degrees earn significantly higher incomes than those without. A college-educated person is more likely to be able to ensure their own economic security, which in turn allows them to see people like them as potential friends rather than as competitors.

This might all sound groovy to your average liberal Democrat. If college completion rates have grown over time, and college reliably moves people to the left, then the outcomes are all to the good, right? Unfortunately, the increasing embrace of the Democratic Party by the college-educated has been matched by a desertion of the party by white voters without degrees. As Cohn wrote, "rising Democratic strength among college graduates and voters of color has been counteracted by a nearly equal and opposite reaction among white voters without a degree." The Democratic Party has shed uneducated whites for the college-educated of all races. And this is more or less to plan; before the 2016 election, Chuck Schumer notoriously said, "For every blue-collar Democrat we lose in western Pennsylvania, we will pick up two moderate Republicans in the suburbs in Philadelphia, and you can repeat that in Ohio and Illinois and Wisconsin." I don't need to tell you how that turned out.

This change is particularly troubling for the left for two reasons, one from the perspective of power, the other of philosophy. First, white voters without college degrees are disproportionately valuable in our system because they tend to congregate in low-population rural states—that is, precisely the states that result in overrepresentation in our Senate, where both the forty million voters of California and the six hundred thousand voters of Wyoming are represented by two senators. Losing white uneducated voters in battleground states like Ohio and Pennsylvania in favor of more college grads in safe blue states like California and New York is a losing game for Democrats.

For the left, the philosophical wound may be even deeper: the left has always stood for the masses over the elites, the workers over management, for the common (hu)man. And, I would argue, the nearly complete takeover of the Democratic party intelligentsia—its political and policy apparatus—by the college-educated illustrates the core divide within left politics itself. Without its fundamental orientation toward elevating the downtrodden, what unites the left's project? We have a coalition, of the college educated and Black and women voters and a large-but-declining portion of Hispanics. But as the Democratic party and liberalism become more and more oriented toward the mores of the college educated—and more and more beholden on policy toward nonprofits and think tanks— we lose the basic coherence that animated the left-of-center in its heydays (the labor movements of the 1910s and 1920s, the New Deal era, and the social movements of the 1960s).

What makes this tension within liberalism more acute is the uncomfortable fact that the liberal intelligentsia, those who most influence the progressive conversation, sits comfortably within the top half of American earners. According to the Bureau of Labor Statistics, the median income of media and communication workers was $62,340 in 2021. This can be compared to a median income of $48,370 for all workers. But this undersells things. While there are many people in national media who are underpaid, and the profession can be long on prestige and short on dough, it's also the case that the people who do more to set the national political conversation are also those who earn more, and the top 10 percent in the sector earn, on average, $120,590. In academia, according to the *Chronicle of Higher Education*, assistant professors make a median wage of $87,043, associate professors $99,820, and full professors $141,476. Of course, academia is also made up of a large mass of contingent labor that makes terrible money, but those who contribute to the national conversation are largely on the tenure track. Think tank and foundation salaries are likely highly context-dependent, but as almost all such positions require college educations, and positions at such institutions are routinely filled by ex-journalists and professors, we can assume the median salaries are equally above the national average.

It's striking: a liberal intelligentsia made up of striving types who mostly attended exclusive colleges and earn attendant higher incomes and yet who largely accept a political philosophy associated with a more fatalistic view on bootstraps and success. Those who set the tenor of the left-of-center conversation do so after having worked hard and climbed the socioeconomic ladder according to principles that they seem to deride in their cultural commentary. They espouse a philosophy based on an assumption of an external locus of control while living lives that presume an internal locus of control. They live according to the bootstraps they disdain in their explicit politics.

This might seem like a mere curio were it not for the (yes, structural) ways that our striving class pulls up the ladder. The trouble is not merely that our liberal intelligentsia has a conflicted relationship with their own locus of control, but that they do so while living lives that deepen the inequalities they abhor.

Consider Richard Reeves's 2017 book, *Dream Hoarders*, which depicts the ways that (despite their egalitarian pretenses) the left-leaning educated upper-middle class has pulled up the ladder behind them and prevented others from ascending the socioeconomic totem pole. As Reeves shows, with their choices in schooling, where to live, and consumption, the top fifth in the American income spectrum effectively close the door behind them on their way up our class system. They do so by taking most of the scarce number of seats at elite colleges, which largely refuse to increase class sizes despite growing population; through hoarding wealth in the form of their homes, homes they purchased thanks to generous home-ownership subsidies and tax breaks in our system; and through what they pass on to their children, literally in terms of inherited wealth but also through those same internal values of hard work and belief in internal locus of control. Reeves's central conceit in his book is that we should pay more attention to the top 20 percent, rather than to the top 1 percent, when we consider America's spiraling inequality problems. But this definition ensnares most of the people who set the progressive agenda.

On issues of race too, tensions haunt the liberal project. The chattering class in media and academia decries racial inequality while occupying fields that are whiter than the country writ large. In our university system, 76 percent of faculty are white, compared to less than 60 percent of the country and 55 percent of undergraduate students. According to the News Leaders Association's Newsroom Diversity Survey, 21.9 percent of salaried workers in newsrooms were people of color in 2019, in comparison to about 40 percent of the country. Meanwhile, only 11 percent of top editors in the American news media are nonwhite, so leadership has an even bigger disparity. Hard numbers on the diversity of think tanks are hard to come by, but the 2020 "Think Tank Diversity Action Statement," signed by hundreds of individuals and endorsed by many of the biggest think tanks and foundations in the country, argued that the field was far too white and required more diversity. These are the fields that have produced reams upon reams of arguments that our country needs more racially diverse representation, particularly among leadership.

So what we're left with when we consider the people who create our liberal narratives are strivers who question the value of striving, affluent critics of affluence whose behaviors deepen economic inequality, and white people who are arch critics of whiteness. All political groups have their own internal tensions and petty hypocrisies, but the liberal intelligentsia is at war with itself.

LOVE ME, I'M A LIBERAL

Back in 1966, the folk singer Phil Ochs recorded a song called "Love Me, I'm a Liberal." In the time period when the 1960s were becoming *the 1960s*, the radical Ochs depicted the hypocrisy and fundamental cowardice of the American liberal. To a remarkable extent, his complaints are echoed by twenty-first-century socialists and radicals: that liberals embrace moral ends but not the means with which we might reach them; that they call for change but only if it can be achieved through proceduralism; that they know the current order is indefensible but endorse a creeping gradualism that ensures we will live with that order for a long time to come. Reading Ochs's lyrics, I think of nothing so much as the nasty online battles in 2016 between supporters of socialist Bernie Sanders and liberal Hillary Clinton. Ochs depicts liberals are soft-left squishes, the type to endorse diversity in the abstract but to recoil from people of color moving next door and to cheer the anti-communist elements of America's labor movement. In a telling line, he sings, "I cheered when Humphrey was chosen, my faith in the system restored."

Humphrey, here, refers to Hubert Humphrey, Lyndon Baines Johnson's vice president and the moderate choice who denied anti–Vietnam War candidate Eugene McCarthy the nomination. Anti-Vietnam sentiment had contributed a great deal to LBJ's deepening unpopularity and subsequent decision to withdraw from the race himself. Humphrey was in many ways the Hillary Clinton to McCarthy's Bernie Sanders, the safe establishment choice, the "whoa, whoa, whoa, slow down there" choice, the path of incrementalism. And, just like Clinton, Humphrey lost to a scandal-generating Republican with a loose grip on the rule of law. Similarly, Ochs references efforts to chase communists out of the AFL-CIO, America's once-radical umbrella union, highlighting the efforts liberals have taken over the decades to moderate even in the face of our reactionary conservative movement.

I'm more interested in Ochs's refrain—"love me, love me, love me, I'm a liberal." He was surely onto something: *love me* is a core element of the American liberal ethos. There's an eternal desire to please at the heart of American liberalism, which I believe contributes to a certain obsequious attitude toward their political project that casts long shadows over left politics today. All of us want to be welcomed and admired, but there's a desperation among American liberals to demonstrate that they are "one of the good ones." Karl Marx famously wrote of the habits of the petite bourgeoisie, the upper-middle class of his age, which always desired to demonstrate that its elevated station had been earned, deserved. Today's affluent liberals are less likely to (appear to) endorse a "just deserts" philosophy of economics than the upper-middle class of yesteryear, but they appear no less eager to prove that their place is deserved. They wage this effort to justify their position with a different kind of virtue: not that of hard work and frugal living, but political virtue, identity virtue, the virtue of having the right kinds of opinions. And those opinions amount to a benevolent, quietly condescending love for minority identities—the Black, the brown, the gay, the transgender, the Muslim, the disabled.

It's here where we can return to the Resistance yard signs, the Facebook profile pictures endorsing some noble cause, and the television shows and movies with self-consciously diverse casting and progressive themes. Having grown up into a discursive culture where old Protestant values of self-denial and restraint have been replaced by identitarian values of overt support for "the Other," today's progressives embrace a different kind of value-laden signaling. They're still religious; they're simply studying a different catechism.

There's a tension in the project for many or most of them, however; something inherently at odds with itself. The white cis straight able-bodied strivers who power the progressive conversation in this country engage with a curious sort of embarrassment, not entirely unalike the embarrassment that the wealthy of an earlier era felt toward their wealth. This is, I think, a result of the common left-of-center tendency to denounce people categorically—such as white people, men, straight cis people, the able-bodied. Such denunciations are absolutely core to the day-to-day engagement of the left-of-center. Because we are now compelled to see all historical oppressions as structural—and not without cause—the tendency is not to denounce bad men but bad masculinity; not racist individuals but white supremacy; not the rudeness of individual able-bodied people but ableism. And so we have a left culture that denounces in aggregate. The claim is rarely that every white person is individually racist, but that all white people benefit from structural racism; not that every man is a predator, but that all perpetuate patriarchy simply by existing. Which leads us to the self-accusing liberal, and also to the strange way that self-accusation becomes a form of self-exoneration.

While most people are savvy enough not to declare themselves to be "one of the good ones," such as by recounting how many Black friends they have, college-educated progressives nevertheless struggle to let it be known that they are, in fact, one of the good ones, that they have the right values for participation in twenty-first-century elite society. The trouble is that what they are protesting, ostensibly, is themselves, the norm, the majority, the hand of oppression. And so many left-of-center people find themselves in a distinctly unpalatable position: they must act as ostensible antagonists to the groups to which they belong. White liberals must denounce whiteness; male liberals must denounce masculinity; straight cis people must denounce heterosexuality as conventionally lived. This is not an original observation, but I find that this dynamic and its consequences are typically underdiscussed in political life, even by a political media that loves nothing more than to autopsy its own members. White progressive people who denounce whiteness are not all deluded or self-dealing, but it requires some mental gymnastics to be a part of the dominant group that insists that the dominant group must take a step back.

THE POLITICS OF DEFERENCE

How this plays out lies in what both Olúfẹ́mi O. Táíwò and I have separately referred to as a "politics of deference." In 2016, I described the politics of deference as "the political theory that suggests that people of a progressive bent have a duty to suspend their critical judgment and engage in unthinking support of whoever claims to speak for the movement against racism and sexism . . . the common notion that allies should 'just listen.'" The politics of deference compels members of dominant groups (particularly white people) to affect a kind of meekness, an affective stance of showy deference toward people from marginalized groups. It's difficult to see how such deference actually helps to end material oppression, but it can function as a kind of consolation prize—although were I a person of color, white people acting even more weird around me would feel like a funny kind of prize. In his 2022 book, *Elite Capture*, Táíwò (who is Black) defines deference politics as a philosophy which "considers it a step toward justice to modify interpersonal interactions in compliance with the perceived wishes of the marginalized." Táíwò is perhaps more inclined to see something worthwhile in deference politics than I am, but he warns that they can contribute to the elite capture that his book warns against. "In such a game," he wrote, "it is much trickier than we realize to avoid moves that intensify elite capture and other oppressive aspects of our social structure"—because the elite, having been trained in language games throughout their lives and especially in college, have the tools necessary to navigate deference politics in a way that redounds to their benefit. One of the many reasons to look askance at our current language games in progressive politics—the constant deployment of complicated jargon and arguments that have been pre-approved by the liberal crowd—is that this scenario empowers people who have had enough formal education to navigate those choppy waters. In other words, it is the privileged who are most likely to deploy the academic political concept of privilege.

A good example of how these rules play out in real-world spaces is the concept of "progressive stack." Progressive stack describes a common set of rules for discourse in left activist spaces. When various people want to speak in meetings, organizers will put them into an ordered list—the "stack." Traditionally, the first person to raise their hand would be put first in the list, and so on in order. In progressive stack, what determines the order in which people speak is their various identity categories. White men speak last, naturally, unless, perhaps, they're trans. Black women go before white, the able-bodied after the disabled. In my experience, this is less tendentious than it sounds. I've been in many meetings where progressive stack was ostensibly the rule, and yet I can't think of a time where it really produced controversy. For one thing, most people don't want to speak most of the time, and when there are only one or two people looking to speak, it's easy to let them while preserving the superficial attachment to diversity and elevating marginalized voices. But progressive stack still functions as a particularly stark statement on the progressive belief in a hierarchy of oppression, the rock-paper-scissors perspective on marginalization and suffering. Some people are on top of the hierarchy, and some are on the bottom, and if we take the ideology at face value, this hierarchy is a perfect inversion of who has power in contemporary American society. White people should be placed on the bottom, in our community of the good, because they are on top.

Progressive stack is a formal policy that's enforced only in specific contexts. But I would argue that liberal discourse norms have created a kind of implied progressive stack whenever politics are debated, and this is what I mean by the politics of deference. We may not regulate the order in which we speak, but savvy progressives know to argue less forcefully and with greater care when arguing with someone who is identified as being part of a more oppressed group. "I'm going to sit my white ass down and listen" is a Twitter cliché, and an odd statement, given that it is an expression of someone who ostensibly does not want to express. This all creates a bit of a dilemma for our white liberals. How do they engage in a politics that supposedly wants them to "lean back"? They need to signal that they're the right kind of person, but signaling fills the air—"takes up space," to use the social justice nomenclature. How do they square this circle?

Not by sitting down and listening, I can tell you that much. Certainly there is some subsection among them that keeps quiet as a matter of deference politics, and they are easy to forget precisely because they stay quiet. But a quick glance at elite media and academia will reveal that there are many people from dominant groups who both believe that their group is overrepresented and yet never stop talking themselves. They resolve this conflict, or attempt to, by being self-critical, by expressing a knowing and apologetic attitude toward their own expression. They keep talking, tweeting, writing essays, and posting YouTube videos, but they layer on provisos and qualifications when they do so. "I know that as a white person I benefit from systemic racism, and that is why you're hearing me," they will say in one way or another before saying what they have to say. "I know that the last thing the world needs is another opinion about abortion from a man," they will say, right before delivering one. Liberals from dominant groups lard their social media with preemptive and perfunctory self-criticism, and then move on to saying what they really feel. This is how we got the group I have called the Good White Men, white male progressives who, thanks to their jaundiced view of white men, are empowered to complain about them as a class, despite it being their own class. They feel no compunction about blaming whiteness and masculinity for all manner of life's problems, and to argue that white men should take a step back, from their positions of high visibility and large audiences.

Sometimes there's naked self-interest at play here. A white man who wants to ascend to a higher-paid leadership position at a left-leaning nonprofit will be sure to mind his p's and q's in how he speaks about race, gender, and sexual orientation. Women in progressive spaces have long complained about men who adopt aggressively feminist personas out of a perceived desire to score with feminist women. And certainly in fields with volatile labor markets like media and academia, where networking and reputation are so core to who succeeds professionally, the rewards for toeing the social justice line are considerable. Still, I think for most performative white liberals the reward is more ephemeral: it's the reward of thinking of oneself as a good person.

If they're sincere in believing that dominant groups are to blame for our problems, and they take care to include themselves as "part of the problem," what's the issue with white male straight cisgender able-bodied people speaking out against the injustice they perpetuate simply by existing? The trouble is that *speaking out as a member of a group about that group's destructive effect is inherently self-exonerating.* Any good white man who publicly takes a stand for the marginalized risks very little— they are saying what their peers want them to say, after all—and stands to gain an implicit place as someone outside of the very critique they're making. They will of course not come right out and say that, as a Good White Man or similar, their critique does not refer to them. But gaining laurels for being the right kind of person from majority identities is an inevitable by-product of towing the identity politics line. Standing up and saying "I stand for the side of good" can't help but cast you in relief with people who don't stand up. Saying that whiteness itself is the enemy, from a standpoint of whiteness, works to distance you from the very categorical critique you're making, no matter how many self-indicting asides you make. It's inevitable. As Nietzsche wrote, "He who humbleth himself wishes to be exalted." Self-criticism must always be, at least to a degree, self-exculpatory. And if we take the maximalist approach to indicting entire classes of people, self-criticism undoes the ostensible intent of (say) a white person complaining about white people entirely. Such a condition inherently implies the existence of the exception to the stated rule.

You might say that this critique is untenable; you're asking people to fail to express their political beliefs on issues of importance and controversy; you're asking white liberals to unilaterally disarm during a culture war. But this confuses where exactly my criticism lies: I don't think apologetic white liberals should cease being publicly liberal. I think apologetic white liberals should cease being publicly apologetic. My frustration does not lie with the concept of muscular political engagement but with the hypocrisy of engaging in it while simultaneously saying that you yourself should "shut up and listen." Those who believe that white people take up too much "space" in the discourse should, indeed, stop taking up such space by shutting up. But the problem there is that they have conceived of this bizarre and unhelpful conception of taking up space in the first place. The idea of taking up space implies a zero-sum game between races, genders, and similar, precisely the kind of political thinking that suggests that the only way for one identity group to flourish is for another not to. But as I have argued in this book, zero-sum racial (or gender, et cetera) thinking is the enemy of progressive politics. White people make up 70 percent of the electorate; men half of it. Straight people, cisgender people, and the able-bodied make up dominant majorities. To convince those people that they must lose for those from marginalized communities to succeed is politically suicidal. As well as wrong: when progress comes, it will come for all of us. White people and men should feel free to contribute to that shared prosperity, even if in doing so they "take up space," because the goal is not to give the marginalized some sort of elevated social status as the most nobly oppressed but to improve the material conditions of all, especially those who have suffered under historical oppression. I don't know if you've looked at the internet lately, but it's big. It's very, very big—big enough for anyone who wants to speak out to do so.

None of these theatrics are new. White guilt is the precursor to the self-abnegating rituals of today's elite progressives, and it's been flourishing since the civil rights era. "Since the '60s," the Black conservative author Shelby Steele said in 2006, "white Americans have been grappling with the stigma, trying to prove that they are not racist, to prove the negative." And in the ensuing decades, that guilt has done very little to actually close the gaps between the living standards of white and Black America. If left materialism means anything, it should mean that leftists should know how little these emotive social mores amount to. And since speaking out against injustice violates the self-flagellating assumptions that are baked into the mores of contemporary white liberals, those assumptions should simply be tossed aside. Black people, women, the gay and transgender, the disabled—they're not crying out for the dominant classes to speak to them with their eyes studying the floor, or to be cynically "elevated" in discursive spaces that progressives control with no referent to material reality. They have specific policy needs and political demands, and meeting them will require the active involvement of the establishment. It's time to drop the theatrics of self-criticism.

Of course, white liberals should remain cognizant of the way that their voices can dominate the conversation. Of course, liberal men should remain cognizant of the tendency of men to speak over others and in doing so silence women's voices. Of course, straight cisgender liberals should be aware of the history of queer erasure in our discourse. But once they are so enlightened, they should then engage without restriction or apology. What's required is not to silence oneself or to engage in the cringe-inducing self-flagellation that's so common to liberal discourse.

Rather, what's required is to reinvigorate the basic rules of conversation that should pertain to everyone, regardless of the dictates of identity politics. Personally, in my own role as someone who debates politics every day, and as someone with a great deal of experience in activism, I understand that the argumentative space is subject to all manner of identity-based inequalities. I also understand that it's unpleasant for everyone and not conducive to hashing out difficult disputes. I have no fetish for civility, and I understand that the powers that be can enforce a certain vision of politeness to further their own ends. But the most straightforward way to ensure that Black people and women and assorted other groups aren't silenced, shouted down, or spoken for is to create a discourse that's more careful, more welcoming, and lower stakes for all. At present, with culture war so overpowering and so many people insisting that the personal is the political, any random utterance can be construed to be an existential, all-defining statement of self; certainly, there are those who have been taken to task by thousands of strangers because of offhand discussion of movies they watched or mundane offline interactions they had. When the reputational stakes always seem artificially high, there's no space to be creative or challenging for any of us. And the insiderism and patronage that are so deeply ingrained in media, politics, and academia can't help but create a discursive system of haves and have-nots, potentially deepening historical inequality in who can influence the conversation. Of course we need to pay special attention to how race or gender silences some. But a more open and constructive discursive space for all of us is the only way to achieve greater discursive equity.

I want affluent liberals—society's progressive winners—to feel free to participate in the conversation, without apology. I want that because ultimately we need them. I have chopped up this group in various ways in this chapter, but however we want to define them, our college-educated, upwardly mobile liberals are a core element of today's left-wing coalitions, probably *the* core element. I've already discussed how essential the votes of college-educated whites have become to the Democratic Party. And for all of their petty hypocrisies, for their naked desires to be seen as the right sort of people, for their tendency to talk of socioeconomic equality while they hoard opportunity, and for their annoying righteousness— there's no future for a better, freer, more equitable America without their participation. They will have to do a lot of the heavy lifting. This text amounts to a book-length argument that the left can and must regain standing among the uneducated and the working class, including the white working class, as the kind of majorities necessary to secure the type of social democratic state I'm after requires their numbers. I also think that the face of the progressive left being some college-educated elite in a tony neighborhood in an expensive city is an insult to what the left has always stood for: the triumph and dignity of the common man.

But you go to war with the coalition you have, not the coalition you wish you had. And perhaps too often in my career I let it go without saying: identity-obsessed liberals who support abortion rights and raising the minimum wage and a sensible immigration policy are far better than the reactionaries that populate the Republican Party. I do think that we can make inroads and peel some of the low-information GOP voters off from that party, but as a leftist I understand that the basic task ahead of me is to turn liberals into leftists, and to help them change their orientation from symbol and language toward the concrete and material realities of our economic and political systems. Surely there are some affluent liberals who would, when push comes to shove, act in their own economic best interest and support a stingier, lower-tax system than the kind that would make single-payer health care and universal pre-K possible. But in general, such people represent the lowest-hanging fruit. If they're more interested in putting up Black Lives Matter signs than in building a coalition that serves all working people, it's only because of the strange and unfortunate cultural moment they find themselves in.

Affluent liberals will go on living in Park Slope and Lincoln Park and Georgetown, piling their lives with the ephemera of social justice, and they will go on obsessing over the right language to use while the right wing makes policy grabs on issues that have teeth. But if we can help these liberals to see their common cause with the working-class voters they tend to disdain, and show them that the best defense against racism and sexism is through building that kind of coalition, they can be powerful allies for our work. To convince them, we will have to rehabilitate the leftist tradition of seeing economic class as the deepest and most salient organizing principle of politics.

7

WHY IS CLASS FIRST?

There's an insult I've heard for most of my political life. My own history with the term goes all the way back to the early days of my self-identification as a Marxist, in my late adolescence, but the term has become more and more common in the years that have followed the 2016 Democratic primary between Hillary Clinton and Bernie Sanders. It's a term that would be alien to the vast majority of ordinary people and is usually confined to internecine squabbles among the left-leaning, and yet it refers to debates that have real political stakes. In a progressive discourse increasingly fixated on categorizing others into tiers of righteousness, it's an insult that suggests cluelessness, ignorance, and casual racism: "class-first leftist."

The term is a pejorative, and has been used to imply a failure to properly "center" minority identity narratives, a privileged myopia about the source of real injustice. A class-first leftist puts class first, which is to say, identifies socioeconomic need and poverty as the locus of progressive organizing. What's wrong with that, you might ask, given that left-leaning politicians and activists have emphasized dollars-and-cents issues for centuries? What's wrong with it, according to some, is that to put class first is to put race, sex, gender identity, disability, and similar concerns second. To be a class-first leftist, in this telling, is to fail to be *intersectional*, and there are few more damning criticisms than that among twenty-first-century leftists. In particular, contemporary leftism holds race and racism as the central locus of all political debate. The prototypical—and, in my experience, largely mythical—class-first behavior is to say, "It's not about race." That statement doesn't just reject the race orientation of current progressive mores, but demonstrates a tone-deaf attitude toward others in the progressive culture. And in the 2020s, where the line between the political and the personal has been systematically erased, being tone-deaf is akin to being evil. Class-first leftists aren't merely wrong on matters of doctrine; they create bad vibes.

During that Democratic 2016 primary, Clinton and Sanders came to be seen not just as representatives of two competing wings of the Democratic Party but as archetypes for fundamental questions facing American progressivism. For her part, Clinton worked relentlessly to establish her credibility as an opponent of racism, sexism, and homophobia, and her coming victory (assumed by many, including me, to be in the bag) was represented as a towering victory for feminism.

To rally voters to these causes is of course a noble effort, and given the demographics of the Democratic Party's base, a political necessity. But Clinton's campaign also embodied the excesses and self-parodic elements of this kind of naked appeal to demographic diversity. An indicative tweet from the official campaign Twitter account contained a notoriously bewildering diagram that purported to show how all of the world's various bigotries and oppressions interact with one another. Referencing the tweet, *The Atlantic*'s Clare Foran acknowledged that "Clinton's invocation of intersectionality may broaden popular understanding of the concept." But she also noted that "there's risk of it becoming a meaningless buzzword."

Stung by repeated criticisms about her coziness with the finance industry, she groused that breaking up the big banks would not end racism, almost a caricature of the tendency of identity politics to shield the moneyed and powerful from its critiques. Clinton had spent a life hobnobbing with the wealthy and powerful, including with her opponent Donald Trump, and was now lecturing the rest of us on standing with the marginalized. Of course, Bernie Sanders himself enjoyed a standard of living well above that of the average American, and in general, elite Democrats have had a somewhat tense relationship with their own financial success.

Despite Clinton's clumsy messaging, the Sanders campaign appeared to be legitimately hampered by the insistence that the candidate was insufficiently focused on identity issues. In March 2016, the Clinton campaign tweeted, "It's not enough to talk only about economics. We have to tackle racial, economic, & environmental justice—together," a thinly veiled dig at Sanders's perceived weakness around identity issues. Sanders was dogged by such accusations throughout the primary, and though it's difficult to say how much he was hurt by this narrative, an antagonistic liberal media ran with it, motivated as much by clicks as by the legitimacy of the critique. In January 2016, *The Guardian*'s Hari Ziyad dinged Sanders for his lack of intersectional bona fides, complaining that at a campaign event he "failed to apply what made [intersectionality] so important—the crucial reality that racial and gendered violence intersect—when asked whether the nation was making more progress on racism or sexism." In this, Ziyad was typical of liberal commentators: it wasn't enough for Bernie to talk about issues like racism and sexism, he had to talk about them in a very particular way—and he failed on that score.

A high-profile incident where several Black women activists interrupted one of his events to complain of his supposed inattentiveness to racial issues played right into the hands of Sanders's many opponents within the press. His every press release was meticulously picked over by Clinton fans, including her many supporters in media—indeed, it frequently felt as though the supposedly unbiased news media *was* Clinton's base—and any inartful language was declared to be evidence of a profoundly unenlightened mindset. This critique continued into 2020. For example, former Clinton 2016 staffer Zerlina Maxwell, who is a Black woman, blasted Sanders's campaign kickoff speech, saying, "He did not mention race or gender until 23 minutes into the speech. And just for point of comparison, I looked at Elizabeth Warren's opening speech for example, she mentioned race and discrimination in the first paragraph." As *Reason* magazine pointed out at the time, this wasn't true—he had brought such issues up in the first five minutes—but the critique stuck. As I was a Sanders supporter myself, it will not surprise you to learn that I found the complaints to be baseless and motivated by cynical political motives. But it is the case that they became part of the communal understanding of the entire Sanders movement, and it's also the case that, whether the class-first accusation was effective or not, both the Warren and Sanders campaigns ultimately floundered in large part because of their inability to make inroads with the Black moderates whom many see as the heart of the Democratic coalition.

In the 2020 campaign, Sanders would make a conspicuous effort to better court Black Democrats, but to little avail. While exit polling showed that he retained a strong showing among Hispanic and Asian voters, and dominated with the youth vote, his inability to attract Black voters only grew, and ultimately his 2020 campaign appeared to have fared worse than his 2016 bid. A piece by the neoliberal Brookings Institution looked at election returns and argued that Sanders badly underperformed in 2020 relative both to 2016 and to his advantages in that later contest. "In every one of the 27 primaries and caucuses thus far," the piece asserted, "Mr. Sanders underperformed his 2016 level of support." The Brookings essay specifically suggested that the 2016 primary was more about anti-Hillary sentiment than pro-Bernie feelings, which might explain the decline in his support.

For many, Sanders's failures proved the salience of the class-first critique. The insult would be used often in the years that followed, directed at the Democratic Socialists of America, the "dirtbag left," a constellation of leftist podcasters and writers, and the left flank of American politics in general. The message from the identitarian left has been simple: class-first politics are not just offensive but a political detriment, as a class-first message will never rally the natural constituencies of the left, meaning various minority groups. But I think that story is wrong. I think, in fact, that if we take those various oppressions seriously, the only way to confront them is with a class-first approach to organizing, as emphasizing socioeconomic issues is the only way for a progressive movement to win. And I think a class-first philosophy for left-wing movements ultimately foregrounds, rather than sidelines, traditional oppressions of minority groups. This chapter will make that case.

CLASS FOCUSED, NOT CLASS REDUCTIONIST

To understand why an orientation toward socioeconomic class is the best hope for progressive change, it's essential to distinguish a class-first leftist from another term which, I'm sorry to say, is often used interchangeably: "class reductionist." The class reductionist is the leftist who not only highlights class, seeing class as the major organizing principle of progressive politics, but also thinks that racism and sexism and homophobia and associated ills *are* class problems. The class reductionist is the guy who thinks that, for example, the oppression of Black Americans can be boiled down to their lower average incomes and wealth, or that high-profile police shootings are sparked by economic inequalities alone, rather than the confluence of poverty and race. The class reductionist believes that effective progressive organizing involves minimizing or ignoring racism, sexism, et cetera, under the dubious logic that those identity issues will necessarily prove divisive and serve as distractions from coming together to fight the bosses, the corporations, and the wealthy. So the story goes.

The liberal publication *Salon* published a piece in 2020, in the thick of the primary, that demonstrated the increasing prevalence of the class reductionist claim, titled "How Calling Someone a 'Class Reductionist' Became a Lefty Insult." The piece pointed out that, like many terms employed in political combat, "class reductionist" is used by many but claimed by none. "The label 'class reductionist' is frequently thrown around on the left today," wrote Asad Haider, "but as was once true of the word 'hipster,' it doesn't appear to be a label anyone willingly accepts"— someone redolent of the term "neoliberal," though with very different underlying politics. In my own experience, for most people who use the term, the class reductionist is anyone more likely to discuss economic issues than they are themselves.

The political scientist, activist, and grumpy left critic Adolph Reed summarized the class reductionist critique, in the process of criticizing those who make it, as

> class reductionism is the supposed view that inequalities apparently attributable to race, gender, or other categories of group identification are either secondary in importance or reducible to generic economic inequality. It thus follows, according to those who hurl the charge, that specifically anti-racist, feminist, or LGBTQ concerns, for example, should be dissolved within demands for economic redistribution.

This is a cogent summary, with Reed's typical incisiveness. The *New Republic* essay this quote is drawn from is titled "The Myth of Class Reductionism." Reed's argument in that piece is correct, in the main, but while I would love to say that the class reductionist is fully a strawman, that he's purely a figment of the identitarian imagination, it wouldn't really be true. In a lifetime in left spaces, I've met all kinds of people, including some who misguidedly think that effectively reaching across social classes necessarily involves minimizing the role of identity categories. I am thinking, in particular, of some misguided Marxists I know, all of them older, as well as a few figures from the labor movement. I can say, however, that this stance is thankfully rare, indeed almost unheard of in a sea of identity politics, and Reed's larger point—"the class reductionist canard is a bid to shut down debate"—is almost always correct. Like so many other boogeymen in left discourse, the class reductionist exists for the rhetorical convenience of those who would shove all of their enemies into the same box. Thus disqualified, the floor is ceded to those who want to fixate on every human distinction but the economic. What's frustrating is that the people who complain of class reductionism insist on their own unduly constrictive perspective on the source of our problems even as they complain about the same failing in others. Once the class reductionist is invoked, Reed wrote, "you may safely dismiss your opponents as wild-eyed fomenters of discord without addressing the substance of their disagreements with you on policy proposals."

The reference to policy proposals is key. A common critique of identity politics (a term, I will remind you, that I use with some misgivings) is that they typically fail to coalesce into specific, material goals, instead tending to result in vague recriminations and assertions of personal bigotries that do not leave us with a clear path of what to organize for and how to fight for it. In *Elite Capture*, Olúfẹ́mi O. Táíwò wrote of this dynamic: "A constructive political culture would focus on outcome over process . . . the pursuit of specific goals or end results rather than avoiding complicity in injustice or promoting purely moral or aesthetic principles." As I discussed in previous chapters, the lack of specific policy aims was a major problem for the 2020 "uprising," ensuring that the immense outpouring of public support had no particular place to go. The class reductionist could be forgiven for looking at the empty sloganeering that so often attends identity-based politics and concluding that such politics are inherently unserious.

In 2018, Francis Fukuyama argued that identity politics had become something of a default frame for global politics—not just on the left but on the right as well.

> Politics today, however, is defined less by economic or ideological concerns than by questions of identity. Now, in many democracies, the left focuses less on creating broad economic equality and more on promoting the interests of a wide variety of marginalized groups, such as ethnic minorities, immigrants and refugees, women, and LGBT people. The right, meanwhile, has redefined its core mission as the patriotic protection of traditional national identity, which is often explicitly connected to race, ethnicity, or religion.

Fukuyama goes on to argue that identity politics has been driven by globalization, which Fukuyama has always vocally championed. Though globalization has resulted in great increases to economic growth (and corporate profits), some have fallen far behind, such as those American workers whose jobs in manufacturing and industry were lost to offshoring. This has deepened identity grievance, in Fukuyama's eyes, causing people to splinter into more and more specific identity categories in a way that makes cooperative problem-solving impossible.

The trouble is that class politics are not inherently any more serious or strategic. After all, Occupy Wall Street and the broader milieu of post–financial crisis activism was relentlessly class focused and yet suffered from a similar lack of structure and demands—the famous refusal of

Occupy leaders to craft a set of demands, the inability to move beyond an inchoate and emotive set of complaints about the elites. I've already discussed the October 2011 *New York Times* piece that summed up the state of Occupy's directionlessness with its headline "Protesters Debate What Demands, if Any, to Make." As previously mentioned, protesters at the time routinely denied the salience of goals and demands under the theory that to demand and be rebuffed would be demoralizing. (Occupy was a very vibes-based movement.) Unconsidered, apparently, was the possibility that demands will prove to be empowering because someone else might in fact respond—that protesters might win, that they might succeed in the work of politics. Either way, Occupy represents a perfect example of how a class-forward politics can be perfectly divorced from considerations of results, in just the way that is commonly alleged of identity politics.

Looking beyond Occupy, this class-based but empty rhetoric can be readily observed on social media, where there's a constant chorus of complaining left voices that make ostensibly class-focused arguments but which are free of political maturity or substance. Twitter is filled with accounts with the hammer and sickle in their bios and ignorance of basic left doctrine in their tweets. I think class-first politics are our only hope, but there's nothing inherently more serious or argumentatively responsible about class-first politics. The Bernie Sanders candidacies represented a far more grounded and pragmatic vision of left engagement than you typically find; that so many of the braying "leftist" accounts think that they are continuing the legacy of those campaigns by getting into meaningless internecine wars online only demonstrates that the most down-to-earth political tendencies can be hijacked in the name of fashion.

It's easy to dismiss identity politics for a lack of tactile goals and an aversion to using the actual levers of power. The broader issue, put simply, is that racism and sexism and homophobia really are unique and uniquely pernicious, they can be lessened but not erased through economic means, and members of disadvantaged groups have every right to expect their particular issues to be given significant weight by a broader liberatory movement. We must be class focused without being class fixated, which is precisely why it's so essential to distinguish class-first politics from class reductionism. I reject the latter label. I embrace the former. It's important to remember: a common complaint against identity politics from the more class focused is that identity politics are insufficiently *material*, that is, that they fail to reference concrete real-world issues and don't seek to change them. When those practicing identity politics fixate on language norms or fulminate over whether enough Oscars are being won by filmmakers of color, critics are correct to see a kind of failure, given how little we'd win even if we had every success possible in those arenas. But what some critics of identity politics fail to understand is that race *is* material. Sex and gender inequality are material. Sexual orientation and gender identity are material. Few things could be more material than disability. Attending to injustices concerning these markers is not inherently a failure to be material; it's only the expression of such politics that can fall into that trap. What we who are class focused must labor to do, then, is not to deny that identity issues are material but to insist that fixation on symbolism is a dead end, is a kind of anti-politics.

One salient difference between class-first and class reductionist is that some people (like me) willingly claim the mantle of the former, while no one professes to be the latter. As Haider wrote in the previously mentioned *Salon* piece, the class reductionist is like the hipster—a creature that seems to exist only in the abstract, a clumsy approximation of some real dynamics that draws in so many people who are guilty of the charge that the term becomes, functionally, a slur. Haider's essay is cogent, but he demonstrates a common tic in these debates: in a likely bid to appear reasonable, several times he asserts that class reductionism is real and a genuine problem, without citing any specific figures or quotes. I have already conceded class reductionism is not an entirely mythical phenomenon. But this tendency to refer generally to class reductionism as a problem without defining who precisely is guilty of it and how many of them there are simply helps those who use the critique insincerely for their own political ends.

Yes, it's possible for any of us to become so focused on issues of monetary and economic inequality that we fail to give adequate consideration to oppressions of race, gender, sexual orientation, and disability. But there are two things I feel I must point out. The first is that we ourselves decide what we're focused on as a movement, what the horizons of our particular project are, and if we are responsible and speak and act with care, there is absolutely no reason that we would have to become myopic in our understanding of injustice. The fear that focus on class will push us over the edge into ignoring issues of race or gender or similar seems to be based on the strange assumption that we do not control our own movements, that they operate outside of our control. But we *are* our movements; they are only us, can only be us, and if we speak and act carefully, we can ensure that identity-based oppressions remain core to our priorities. More, I simply cannot look out at the current state of the American left-of-center and conclude that the problem is insufficient focus on racial or gender issues. Liberal discourse in the 2020s is absolutely obsessive about these dynamics; there is no reason to fear that we will suddenly forget them.

COMMON CAUSE, OR NOT

If we recognize that there is a danger of becoming too fixated on class, however small, we should also recognize that there are great opportunities in using class as the central organizing vehicle for progressive politics. Among other advantages, class issues are universal, where identity politics by their very nature can appear limited and exclusionary, as they speak to conditions that are by definition shared by minorities of the population.

The universality of class politics is core to Marxism and thus to the left politics of the past two hundred years. "According to Marx," the philosopher and political scientist Renzo Llorente once wrote, "the proletariat constitutes a 'universal class', namely a class whose particular interests are identical to the general interests of society." The proletariat is the working class, which is to say, the class that labors; they survive by trading their labor power for wages. In the Marxist analysis, this trade is fundamentally unbalanced and unfair—the workers create the value that makes society run, but a small parasitic class captures that value and gives the workers a small fraction of it in exchange. While much has changed in the century and a half since Marx's heyday, this basic reality has not changed. Most people, and most of any group within the broader population, earn their money through this exchange of work for inadequate wages. The portion of society that instead makes money on the other side of that equation remains very small. For this reason, organizing around the concept of work and labor, and performing outreach to those who work *as people who work*, represents the broadest and most universal type of appeal and thus the best possibility for mass politics.

"In defending and pursuing its interests this class also defends and pursues the interests of society as a whole," wrote Llorente.

What too often goes undiscussed in left spaces in the social justice era is this: While the act of dividing the left's constituencies into smaller and smaller identity niches might be fine for academic analysis, it's ruinous for taking action. Ruinous because the smaller and smaller you slice humanity into groups, the less power those groups have, whether that be the power of votes, of organizing, or of educating the masses. As the socialist historian Eric Hobsbawm wrote, "Winning majorities is not the same as adding up minorities." Ideally, we would love it if we could effectively appeal to the masses by making reference to the needs of others, but both political science and human experience tell us that we must make people understand how their own needs are advanced with our preferred action. Ordinary people join political movements when they feel they have common cause, which is to say, shared self-interest. They naturally ask, "What's in it for me?"

That might sound crude or selfish, like Ayn Rand's political philosophy of objectivism, but it's only a simple statement of how most people interact with the world. And as it happens, radical-left traditions such as Marxism have always accepted the preeminence of self-interest. ("Individuals have always started out from themselves," states Marx in *The German Ideology*, "and could do no otherwise.") For our movements to fixate relentlessly on markers of difference rather than shared needs is to undercut the most basic appeal the left has: that what's good for some of us is what's good for all of us. These dangers of identity fixation are particularly pernicious given the identitarian left's current obsession with "centering," with putting certain groups first, giving them preferential position as the most important elements of our coalition. This kind of showy philosophy of the greater priority of the most oppressed may be easily adopted by the numerically tiny number of college-educated liberals who now dominate our political discursive spaces, but will never attract the masses, who like all of us spend most of their days wondering how to care for themselves and their families.

That is not, of course, to say that we shouldn't consider combatting racism or sexism or homophobia to be special priorities. Of course they must be, if we are to pursue real justice. But it's one thing to recognize them as distinct and unique problems, and to understand the profound evil they represent, and another to tell those from outside any one of those particular groups that their problems are therefore not problems. The messaging tweaks that ensure that we maintain the former while avoiding the latter are not complicated. But the left-of-center must contend with a self-inflicted wound, which is endless, incessant fights over whether any individual is adequately prioritizing those who are seen as the most oppressed. Here we return to the politics of deference—the assumption that left-leaning people must undertake a kind of identity triage and showily place the needs of minority groups over others, often in a way that has little or no reference to specific policies or actions. Táíwò wrote, "To opt for deference, rather than interdependence, may soothe short-term psychological wounds. But it does so at a steep cost: it may undermine the goals that motivated the project—and it entrenches a politics that does not serve those fighting for freedom over privilege, for collective liberation over mere parochial advantage."

There is nothing wrong with maintaining identity groups within part of a broader coalition. But those groups themselves are inevitably defined not by a shared struggle to achieve specific goals but by a kind of victim insiderism. What's more, a coalition that is made up of these smaller identity groups will always be at war with itself, as the specific groups jockey for position and demand outsize deference from other members. This can clearly be seen with the advent of "affinity groups," which are found on college campuses and in activist circles but also increasingly within corporate structures. And these groups have proven time and again to produce angst and division rather than unity. I myself have seen the damage that they can do on several occasions, as the demand that a specific slice of a coalition be prioritized above others results in infighting, recrimination, and understandable resentment from those who have been told that their needs are not a priority.

Putting the demands of small groups within larger movements ahead of the good of the movement itself can have real-world negative impact. The story, as it was told to me, was that in 2019, a New York–based chapter of the Democratic Socialists of America planned to canvass in the city for Medicare for All. This would seem to be a very natural combination of tactics and messaging for a socialist organization; Medicare for All has emerged as the signature left-wing policy demand of the post-Sanders-candidacy left, and door-knocking to spread the word about a candidate or issue has long been a core tactic of left activist groups. And this issue would seem to be especially important to the disabled, who stand to gain much in an America with a sensible and humane medical system. But this simple plan to do outreach for a vital issue was torpedoed when members of DSA's disability caucus caught wind of the plan. New York has many walk-ups, that is, apartment buildings without elevators. These loud voices within DSA (mostly on Twitter) demanded to know what accommodation the organizers of the canvassing event would make in the event that a wheelchair-bound member wanted to participate. (To my knowledge, such a person remained theoretical throughout the controversy.) The organizers of the canvassing event could of course do nothing to accommodate such members; it's unfortunate that so many of New York's apartment buildings are older and do not have elevators, but changing that would be beyond the power of any group. You might hope that this simple logic would win the day, but it was not to be. These members (who defined themselves, it seems, as part of the disability caucus ahead of being members of the larger group) caused such a loud and angry ordeal on social media that the plan to canvass was quietly scrapped, and dozens or hundreds of potential supporters of Medicare for All went unreached.

To a degree, this is merely an artifact of the unhealthy internal politics of a specific leftist group, albeit a large and influential one. But the scenario was also a perfect encapsulation of the problem with "put us first" politics; sometimes, for a movement to flourish, the movement itself must be prioritized above its constituent parts. A coalition that is driven first and foremost by the demands of the individual fiefdoms within it is a marriage of convenience, and like all such marriages it will break down when the going gets tough. And the tragedy lies in the self-defeating nature of these dynamics. The demand to make accommodations for the disabled is righteous, but if a disability "affinity group" sabotages its larger organizing vehicle, they will never be empowered to actually effect positive change for disabled people or anyone else. The fundamental question is whether the specific identity groups work to serve a broader movement for justice that can potentially give those groups what they want when empowered, or whether the arrow points in the other direction and the identity groups glom on to the broader movement only in the hopes of leveraging their own needs and desires. The latter cannot be a winning political strategy, as the cacophony of conflicting demands will always result in incoherent political action and failure.

For the record, the aforementioned situation with DSA and the supposedly ableist canvassing action does not reveal a problem with the concept of special accommodation for the disabled, but with a failure to recognize what reasonable accommodation entails. That is the legal standard demanded by the Americans with Disabilities Act: that employers, schools, public buildings, and sundry other human institutions extend every reasonable accommodation to the disabled. The demand to install ramps for entry to public buildings is reasonable. The demand to give students with learning disabilities extra time to take tests is reasonable. Demanding that specific activists somehow be given access to inaccessible public buildings, with no clear means to do so and by an organization with limited resources, was not reasonable. And it is here, I think, that a lot of the messy work of politics must simply be hashed out in the day-to-day scrum of argument: for all minority groups, not just the disabled, there are both reasonable and unreasonable demands for accommodation, for deference. People of conscience must do the work of arguing which is which, and we can be sure that there will be good-faith disagreements in any healthy and diverse group. What's needed therefore is an open and forgiving argumentative space, where people who say that a given demand is not reasonable are not immediately assumed to be acting on behalf of the oppressor, and where those who are demanding more accommodation are not dismissed as selfish or weak.

It's also fair to note that, precisely because the critiques of feminism and civil rights and related schools of thought are correct, these affinity groups cannot hope to achieve the desired change without ceding control to a larger group. That is to say that, yes, women are systematically disempowered in our society; yes, Black people receive political representation that is less than what they should proportionally receive; yes, trans people are a tiny and vulnerable population—and for these exact reasons, the only hope for these groups is to work within a broader coalition to appeal to the masses and grow its people power. Again, I return to the fundamentally self-interested nature of Marxism: the proletariat, the workers, those who don't make a living simply by collecting interest on what they own, are not the basic unit of politics simply because of their inherent dignity or the aesthetics of labor but because they are a constituency that can win. It's hard to remember in a country where the labor movement has been in decline for well over a half century, but the power of unions has never been primarily political, though unions certainly rally their members at the ballot box. The power of unions is fundamentally that they may deny capital their labor power, shutting down the factories and bringing the boss's profits to a halt. Union power is thus fundamentally founded on a kind of direct action, which is why unions don't need to be popular to be effective. What similar power do, say, the disabled have as the disabled? They are a group that demands our attention and support, but they do not have inherent and intrinsic access to a particular type of power by their very nature. The working classes do. This, as much as any other reason, is why we should put class first.

And, yes, effective politics may very well include sublimating the short-term desire for recognition and emotional attention of minority groups to the long-term (and far more meaningful) goal of winning power and, having done so, adopting the policies the members of these groups want. This is particularly important when it comes to matters of race, as a large corpus of political science demonstrates that when a given political demand is embedded in a message of racial justice, that demand becomes less popular than when it is framed in other terms. Reflecting on the tendency within American liberalism to use racial framing when arguing for programs that are good for everyone (such as raising the minimum wage or clean-air legislation), Marc Novicoff wrote in 2021 that

> the premise of this style of argument seems to be that there are lots of people who are skeptical of race-neutral social welfare programs who will become more enthusiastic about them when the policies are framed as winners for racial equity. . . . [But] data clearly supports that this framing is counterproductive—almost everyone who cares a lot about racial justice also supports an expanded welfare state, whereas *lots* of people who support progressive economic policies have conservative views on racial justice questions.

It's of course lamentable that many American voters see racial framing as a turnoff, but that it's lamentable doesn't change the fact that it's true. And it's essential to see the alternatives presented: if we minimize divisive racial messaging and in so doing win support for policies that ultimately help racial minorities, we've achieved the material goal; if we emphasize race in our messaging and lose voters in the process, we may sound righteous, but we accomplish nothing. Again, it's worth considering what it means for politics to be *material*: racial inequality is profoundly material, but purely linguistic victories do not have material consequences. What difference does it make if Black people are "put first" in some entirely symbolic way, if no coalition large enough to actually improve their living conditions is built?

We might ask what historical examples we have of identity-first groups succeeding in changing the world; they appear to be thin on the ground. (Part of the issue is that progressives have such a fundamentally pessimistic take on identity issues these days that they don't want to acknowledge any victories at all, which means they can rarely speak of the efficacy of their own preferred approach.) In contrast, class-conscious narratives have worked frequently in the past. The American civil rights movement of the twentieth century was of course first and foremost a movement for racial justice, and a fantastically successful one. But it's key to note that it was neither exclusively fixated on racial issues nor exclusionary of people who were not Black. The civil rights movement was, in fact, deeply invested in economic dimensions of human rights and justice, based on the correct assumption that Black Americans could not be truly liberated until they were freed from the bondage of wage slavery and poverty. The famous March on Washington where Martin Luther King Jr. gave his famous "I Have a Dream" speech was, in fact, fully titled the March on Washington for Jobs and Freedom; King's last major political efforts before his assassination were the Poor People's Campaign and lending support to striking public workers in Memphis, Tennessee. King never wavered from a clear commitment to economic justice, nor saw it as separable from racial justice. He recognized that there were special challenges to achieving an economically just society. "Slums with hundreds of thousands of living units are not eradicated as easily as lunch counters or buses are integrated," he wrote in *The Nation* in 1966. "Jobs are harder to create than voting rolls."

It's difficult to see examples of where identity-based groups have effectively motivated even the broader population of people within the named groups. "Without outside compulsion or pressure," Hobsbawm wrote, "under normal circumstances [identity politics] hardly ever mobilizes more than a minority. . . . Attempts to form separate political women's parties have not been very effective ways of mobilizing the women's vote." As extensively discussed in a previous chapter, Black Lives Matter cannot fairly claim to represent the interests of most Black Americans, whom opinion polls show to be in large majorities far more moderate than the activist group.

And so we see that organizing around identity groups cannot possibly succeed at the kinds of scales necessary to create truly transformative societal change, as minority groups suffer from a lack of money, power, and influence, and those that would attempt to speak for such groups never even fully convince those communities to come onboard themselves. The best that can be accomplished is legislation like the Americans with Disabilities Act—a triumph of law, no doubt, but one easily siloed, and no real challenge to the dominance of the powers that be. Basing a broad and multidimensional movement for social justice around the needs of specific demographics—which is to say, based on those needs as defined by the loudest members among them, which is often very far from the actual average opinion—does the devil's work for him. If those loud voices win, they are in effect leveraging their oppressed status for selfish ends; if they fail, they risk isolating the very groups for which they speak.

RIGHT-WING IDENTITY POLITICS

Those who practice identity politics (who rarely claim the term themselves) are quick to point out that the right wing also practices identity politics. And they're quite right. Indeed, in the 2020s, the right seems to have little else than identity politics, having sidelined its traditional emphasis on the Christian identity of the United States in favor of a politics of pure resentment, disdaining one imagined identity (the stereo-typical "woke" liberal, overeducated, sanctimonious, hypocritical, and ignorant) and lionizing another (the all-American, the proudly provincial, the gun-toting, flag-waving defender of traditional values). Right-wing media has precious little to do with policy these days, as the right's biggest stars achieve that status merely by goring the right ox—defining the most over-the-top woke stereotype and skewering it, again and again, creating a kind of anti-politics. Meanwhile Republican politicians use this form of identity politics to win elections and then, when in power, fight for deregulation and lower taxes on corporations, an actual policy agenda that's not even popular among their own voters. As liberals have been pointing out for decades, "white rural patriotic Christian" *is* an identity, no less so than any of those progressives champion, and the fact that those who hold that identity imagine themselves to simply function as the default is precisely what members of disadvantaged groups must organize against. Certainly the identity politics charge indicts the right wing too.

The trouble is that, while this is a clever rejoinder, it doesn't change the underlying political context, and that context is one in which the right is better able to utilize identity politics than the left. The first reason for this is a matter of bare math: though the United States has been diversi-fying steadily over the past century, 70 percent of the electorate remains white, and the inherent undemocratic aspects of the Electoral College and Senate further this advantage. The country has been growing steadily more college-educated over time, and the college-educated are heavily left-leaning, but it remains the case that less than 40 percent of American adults has a college degree. Most worryingly of all, the assumption that a browner United States is necessarily a more liberal United States has recently come into question. Among others, Ruy Teixeira, a political scientist who was one of the first to predict that growing racial diversity in the United States would lead to an enduring Democratic majority, sounded the alarm after the 2020 election and pointed out that Hispanic and Asian voters were not following the script. "Hispanic Voters Are Normie Voters," read one of his headlines, emphasizing that the Hispanic voters who were broadly assumed to reliably vote Democrat are, in fact, subject to the same pressures and biases as any other class of voter. (Even Black men broke toward Trump in greater numbers in 2020 than they had in 2016, though the overall number of Black Trump voters remained small.) What all of this means is that if liberals are playing identity politics with smaller and smaller niches, thanks to their obsession with standing for the marginalized, and conservatives are playing identity politics with white voters without college degrees, the basic electoral math doesn't look great for Democrats.

But the problem is deeper. A large element of the left's intellectual and philosophical development of the past century has been to attack traditional grand narratives like "the American way" or the Enlightenment project or the superiority of a rights-based vision of human flourishing. And it's not difficult to see why a movement focused on securing the rights of oppressed groups might adopt such cynicism about these narratives: they have conspicuously failed to defend the rights of minorities even when they embrace such a defense in the abstract. The trouble is that you have to have something to rally people around—an idea, a symbol, a code—and the left has proven consistently incapable of coalescing around such a vision. This is *especially* problematic if you have already divided up your coalition into an endless number of identity groups and put them on a hierarchy of suffering. The contemporary left-of-center essentially tells potential converts that they are only the demographic groups they belong to and that these groups define their politics (despite, to pick a salient example, the rise of the Hispanic Republican), and that the larger ideals and institutions that we might sacrifice for are merely fictions told by power. Left-leaning people and groups don't want to appeal to patriotism or capitalism or the American way, and I certainly include myself in that distaste as well. But they also want to constantly fixate on difference rather than shared need, leaving them without a clear sense of what to appeal to when addressing the American people, perhaps except for the abstraction of social justice. It's a mess.

I sometimes think about Hillary Clinton's official campaign slogan from 2016, "Stronger Together." This is good politics—it centers the group over the individual, de-emphasizing the candidate relative to her party and supporters, which is especially savvy when that candidate has always been divisive. But of course few people remember this official slogan, as far more prevalent was another—"I'm with Her." This turns the strength of the official slogan on its head and emphasizes the specific candidate over the masses, fronts gender issues above common cause, and sounds narcissistic. In the end, the 2016 campaign became a referendum on the establishment, with Clinton serving as its perfect avatar, a consummate insider running on celebrity glitz and glamour in a period when the country was wracked with economic anxiety. Absent any compelling vision of something greater to fight for, the Hillary Clinton campaign was left with only Hillary, who fairly or not was one of the most unpopular politicians in the history of public polling. And this dynamic dogs the left today: defined by its lists of oppressive -isms, given to endless complaints about everything that's wrong with the world, we are far less able to define a positive vision of what exactly we're fight for and why the world we want is better than the alternative. Surely the right's anti-politics are worse, but as we busily undermine faith, national identity, and all other ways human beings create meaning, we risk standing for nothing and thus losing everything.

If conservatives can continue to base their fundamental message around God, country, and traditional ways of life, even as their worship of Trump functions as a repudiation of such traditionalism, how can the left rally its many distinct parts together to win power and achieve social change? Through class, of course; through the universalizing power of class politics and the plain truth that the interests of the moneyed few are antagonistic toward those of the rest of us.

WE REALLY ARE IN THIS TOGETHER

Writing in *Jacobin*—frequently referred to as America's premier socialist journal—Paul Heideman said in 2019 that "the socialist theory of class says a lot. What it doesn't say, however, is that other forms of oppression don't matter." This common sense notion of "both/and" arguments about class oppression and other forms, as opposed to a facile desire to rank human miseries and the injustices that cause them, seems so obvious that it's remarkable that progressive spaces are so often beset with infighting over whose oppression is the worst. I have long suspected that such fights occupy so much time in the far left because the far left has little power; unable to actually achieve the change we desire in the world, we squabble endlessly over who holds what level of priority in the movement, as this seems like the last laurel we can fight for. But if we ever are to take power, we will have to do so as a coherent and cohesive movement, and I believe the only way to achieve that internal consistency is through appeals to socioeconomic class, on the simple logic that all people worry about money.

We should of course want to cultivate the moral imagination, by which I mean the capacity to think about the suffering of groups we do not belong to, recognize the injustice they face, and resolve to work to end that injustice. But as I've said, politics is the art of self-interest. The foundation of left politics lies in the belief that the politics of personal interest *develops into* a class politics, when people are free of self-delusion. And they develop that way because a self-interested person, if free from the myopia that Marx called false consciousness—the delusion that one controls his own fate and will one day become one of the wealthy masters of the universe—will inevitably come to understand that the only way to win the battle against exploitation is for all the exploited to band together and fight it en masse.

The question thus becomes, what form of exploitation do the most possible people face? And the obvious answer there is socioeconomic hardship. We can't rally people around the needs of racial groups when there are several such groups in our society, particularly given that a majority of the largest among them seems firmly ensconced in the Republican Party. We can't rally people based on gender when society is split about halfway down the middle between cisgender men and women, and with the various other gender identities numerically tiny. We can't rally people around sexual orientation when we don't all share the same sexual orientation, especially given the way that gay identity has ceased to be a politically live issue in and of itself since the legalization of gay marriage. I'm not talking about our priorities and policies as a winning coalition, which will necessarily concern ourselves with the injustices heaped on minorities, but rather about our fundamental appeal to all people. You can't build unity by fixating on difference; it's nonsensical. Instead, you say, "I am not like you, in some important ways, but you and I recognize that we have common cause, and if we can work together we can make the world freer and fairer for both of us." This is the fundamental appeal of all true-left politics.

Everyone has to pay the rent. Almost everyone has lean months and hard years. Many people struggle to afford groceries; everybody, at some stage, feels wronged by the boss but unable to do anything about it. I have my misgivings about the "We Are the 99 Percent" framing that emerged from Occupy; in my first book, I argued that we must pay equal attention to the divide between the bottom 80 percent and the top 20 percent, given the way that the top quintile (my quintile) has pulled away from the rest of the country. But the basic wisdom that impossibly wealthy individuals and institutions have rigged the deck against the common man is as true as it has ever been and represents a great messaging opportunity. And, of course, unlike with the framing of Black people versus the rest, gay people versus the rest, trans people versus the rest, et cetera, the numbers are on our side when we emphasize social class. There's only 1 percent of people in the 1 percent, after all, and the top 20 percent are outnumbered four to one.

Though the United States is the most economically powerful country on Earth, public polling reveals a nation full of people who feel economically insecure, who can't cover the cost of minor emergencies, who think the economy and the country are headed in the wrong direction. Even when majorities respond to such polls positively, the existence of large minorities who are underpaid, unsatisfied, or afraid can be used to stoke the basic human desire for fairness. We don't need to exaggerate the number of people living in poverty to convince the electorate that any number is too high, nor do we need to pretend that everyone is unhappy at work to make the argument that the workplace is a site of exploitation and dissatisfaction. It's worth pointing out that the basic American partisan political situation has been, for decades now, that Democrats have more popular economic policies but less popular social views, while Republicans prefer unpopular economic policies that favor the wealthy but effectively leverage the divisiveness of Democratic cultural issues to win. George W. Bush's "compassionate conservatism" was at its heart a Republican appeal to economic justice, and while he did not govern compassionately, he was able to lead the GOP out of the hard-right economic politics of Reaganism and back into the White House. (Albeit while losing the popular vote.) Donald Trump's economic populism proved to be almost entirely empty, and his signature legislation as president was (of course) a tax cut for the rich. But by promising not to touch Medicare and Social Security, which failed vice presidential candidate Paul Ryan had constantly threatened to do, he helped make himself viable in purple states like Wisconsin and Michigan, which won him the presidency. Meanwhile his opponent appeared to hurt her chances by failing to emphasize the economic populism of her agenda in favor of broad waves to the identity politics endorsed by our chattering classes. Republicans know better than to emphasize their unpopular obsession with cutting taxes on the wealthy, and yet Democrats seem determined to campaign in ways better suited to inspiring positive op-eds in the *New York Times* than in earning votes. The popular economically populist agenda of the Democrats can inspire, as seen in the Bernie Sanders campaigns, but Democratic fealty to "the groups"—the nonprofits and foundations that hire overeducated young staffers who write position papers and lobby—seems to chain them to unpopular identity rhetoric.

Just laying this basic condition out makes me nervous, as referring to the unpopularity of Democratic social positions and hybrid social-economic issues like immigrants invites claims that I am asking the left-of-center to abandon Black people, women, immigrants, and the like. Most absurdly, this kind of talk sometimes results in talk of a "red-brown alliance," the idea that one can win by fusing the economic populism of communism with the hatred of the Other of fascism. (No one advocates for this alliance themselves, mind you, but rather accuse others of advocating it as a way to discredit them.) But those are absurd distractions. There is no contradiction between a strategy of emphasizing shared economic need and protecting minority rights. And the idea is not at all to abandon social issues entirely but to pay careful attention to how they are framed and discussed. Immigration, for example, is a polarizing issue in American life, and polling on broad amnesties or large increases in total immigration typically shows steep resistance, even among traditional liberal constituencies. But more nuanced questions about topics like legal paths to citizenship for those already here tend to poll better, suggesting that the public is at least somewhat receptive on this issue. On abortion, the question of framing and narrative are hugely important. Most Americans believe in a legal right to abortion, but the question is susceptible to framing and often turns on in which week of pregnancy abortions might take place. With the 2022 overturning of the *Roe v. Wade* decision in the Supreme Court, and the subsequent criminalization of abortion in several states, our need to advocate strategically as well as angrily has only grown. The famous dictum that abortion should be safe, legal, and rare has attracted a good deal of ire from feminist activists, and in a vacuum, I agree; my preferences for abortion is that it be safe, legal, and accessed as often as women need to access it. But I recognize that my position is not shared by most of my fellow voters, and an insistence on abortion without apology, rather than a strategic focus on unfettered abortion access, is unlikely to be a political winner. We should want to be moderate and careful in our appeals about the issue while staunchly defending abortion access in practice. After all, if Democrats appearing to be extremists about abortion results in a Republican taking office, then abortion rights will be threatened far beyond any restrictions liberals might agree to on the campaign trail. And the most effective way to defuse such radioactive social issues is by returning the conversation to basic pocketbook issues of economic policy, where the left-of-center has an advantage.

Finally, I must simply assert something, a point of view I won't try to justify with empirical evidence but which I both believe myself and assume most of you reading this believe: I think most people want to come together across difference for the good of all, rather than to be divided into smaller and smaller slices based on identity categories they don't control. Over the past several years, American progressives have begun to reinstitute a pernicious form of segregation. Sometimes this segregation is literal, as when they form those "affinity groups" at school or work, where people are separated out into groups of Black or Hispanic or Asian or gay or trans or disabled or other. This segregation (which is the only honest term for it) is meant to make the members of these groups comfortable. But the very concept is inimical to solidarity, the most basic means and end of left politics. Solidarity requires that we see common humanity, that we recognize shared struggle, that we look at the suffering of another and imagine ourselves in their position and are thus moved to work for better for them. However noble the intent of intersectional politics may be, by fixating relentlessly on the need to stress difference, those who practice them are undermining the capacity for the only tool that might relieve those very oppressions they decry: people power, the formation of a mass movement.

As the American sociologist and left activist Todd Gitlin once wrote, "If there is no people, only peoples, there is no left."

8

TO FIGHT FOR EVERYONE

I'm a Marxist, and though a fairly unorthodox one at this point, I would still love to see a Marxist revolution—you know, an international movement of workers rising up and taking control of the political and economic systems, distributing resources and labor based on need and organized under the principle of shared ownership of the productive apparatus of society. This appears to be an unrealistic dream, for now, so I'm left to piece together a set of lefty policy preferences that I can live with, the same as anyone else—a child tax credit, far more muscular laws protecting labor organizing, single-payer health insurance, reparations for slavery, and so on.

Anyone can give you a list of political goals, and whether they succeed or not is usually out of our hands. This chapter is not going to be a list of policies that I want to see implemented or laws that I want to see passed—not predominately, at least. If I mention specific positions that I prefer, it is, I hope, in service of more general principles about how to think and act politically in this fallen world. What I am laying out here is less what I want and more how I think people who want what I want should go about getting it. Like all advice, it's freely given and you can take it or leave it.

RETURN TO ORGANIZING ALONG CLASS LINES

The last chapter explains the reasoning of such a shift at great length. But what does that mean in concrete terms? It involves reprioritizing the labor movement in progressive discourse, and it involves making appeals to people as members of an economic class in a way that can be uncomfortable for today's progressive intelligentsia.

Reinvigorating the labor movement has been a proposed fix for the left's problems for so long that calling for it is a cliché. Organizations like the Democratic Socialists for America and journals like *Jacobin* call for it; Bernie Sanders works it into his speeches; left podcasters present it as one of the basic requirements of a reborn American left. There have been some high-profile victories, such as nascent efforts to organize Starbucks workers and other service-sector employees. But for most of us, organized labor remains stubbornly abstract, as the percentage of workers who are part of a labor union now stands at about 10 percent. I myself was part of a large labor union for four years, the American Federation of Teachers, and enjoyed going to my chapter meetings and demonstrating for better contracts. But for most Americans, particularly the kind of college graduates who produce most left-wing commentary, the labor movement is very far from their lived experience. Unions have been in retreat for so long that many people have no family members who have participated in them. And that in turn makes it harder to imagine their rebirth.

But we can't give up on labor organizing. Labor unions have long been the closest thing to a counterweight that our system has to corporate influence in politics; unions can raise money and lobby in a way similar to moneyed interests and will (theoretically, at least) pull the Democrats left in the same way that corporate lobbies pull them right. Second, labor unions have ways to press for change that are not strictly political. A strike, for example, is fundamentally not a political tool—its purpose is not to attract the support of the people but rather to force an employer to make concessions by denying the labor necessary to make profit. This kind of direct action is extremely valuable to left-wing causes, as it can enable progressive change without the need to win public opinion. Most important for our interests here, unions have traditionally been a means of organizing that cut across racial and ethnic lines. Obviously, shared participation in a union does not eradicate bigotry, and there is an igno-minious history of unions perpetuating racial inequality. But it's also true that, at their best, labor unions have helped workers (mostly men) of different racial backgrounds see their shared interest as workers. This solidarity could never fully erase racial division, but it could convince people that their similar needs could unite them around common pur-pose. Once they recognized that, racial reconciliation (while it would be nice) would not strictly speaking be necessary.

This is a model for what left-leaning people should pursue writ large—hoping for a deeper sense of brotherhood across lines of iden-tity, but prioritizing a less-ambitious culture of shared self-interest and working together. As I said though, the labor movement has been on the ropes for a long time. Reviving it will take a vigorous pursuit of union-friendly laws by the Democrats, who sadly seem lukewarm on the labor movement in general. It will also take a lot of brave people working against entrenched power to organize their workplaces, as we've seen (for example) in recent efforts to unionize Amazon's vast workforce. I'm not equipped to offer a comprehensive plan for how to revive the American union, but I recommend the work of Jane McAlevey, particularly her 2016 book *No Shortcuts: Organizing for Power in the New Gilded Age*.

Belonging to an official organization that's negotiating for a contract shared between workers from different backgrounds is an ideal scenario, but there's no reason we can't adopt those general principles in broader political organizing. In a society that feels more and more atomized by divisions of race and gender and religion and education—thanks in no small part to contemporary progressives, perversely—the appeal of class solidarity can still shine through. Again, not necessarily because of some deeper social reconciliation but because people recognize that in a very deep sense they're in it together, against the wealthy, the corporations, the reactionaries in our government, the system. The community of people who know what it's like to struggle to pay the rent is larger than any racial, gender, ethnic, or religious group.

I can think of two immediate problems with this approach. The first is that the progressive conversation is disproportionately made up of people who don't actually have a lot of experience worrying over how they'll pay the rent. There are, of course, many journalists and writers and pundits and podcasters who are familiar with middle-class-and-below existence. But there's also a great many who aren't, ambitious strivers from upper-middle-class and upper-class families who have Ivy League degrees and who have enjoyed the comforts of material security their entire lives. People like this are profoundly overrepresented among lefty tastemakers, and I suspect that a lot of the resistance that you get to class-first messaging (and the insistence that it's necessarily antagonistic to anti-racism or feminism) stems from those who have never really wanted for anything in their lives. The second obvious problem with class-first messaging is that you do, in fact, have to avoid telling people that their problems aren't problems—you can't effectively reach out to men or white people or Christians by telling them that their needs are subordinate to those of others. Fortunately, you can address issues like racism and sexism and similar as wholly unique and as among the highest priorities of a progressive movement while still effectively engaging in class-first messaging. Unfortunately, a lot of left-leaning people don't agree, and insist we can only put one identity group or the other first. Probably because they can offer them little besides the entirely abstract laurel of being "put first."

I've already discussed why being class-first does not mean being class reductionist. But to reassure you, organizing along class lines does not entail dropping messaging about race, gender, sexual identity, or similar. When the problem is racism, call it racism. Never shy away from confronting racial or gender inequality in explicit and frank terms. But orienting around class lines means using shared economic need as the organizing principle through which we create the majorities necessary to actually *do* something about racism, about sexism, et cetera.

The good news is that Democratic leadership has traditionally been comfortable making fundamentally economic appeals to voters. Joe Biden, for all of his faults, is adept at messaging around economic issues, the policies that might address them, and the people who might benefit from those policies. Unfortunately, these policies are usually entirely insufficient to address the identified economic problem, but at least the muscle memory for addressing pocketbook issues exists within the Democratic Party. Then again, Biden is notoriously old to hold his office, and younger generations of Democratic activists and staffers tend to be believers in the current fashion for insisting that we must ostentatiously put identity issues first. That, after all, was the story of the 2016 Democratic primary, where the old-school class politics of Bernie Sanders were pitted against the purposefully complex intersectionality of Hillary Clinton. What approach wins the day will help determine the future of the left and its success.

TAKE OPPORTUNITIES FOR SOLIDARITY WHERE YOU FIND THEM

The left needs people power. Conservatism wins when nothing changes; the left only wins when things change. The right defends the status quo, and the status quo, politically, is a fortress with very strong walls. The only hope we have to achieve the kind of change we feel is morally necessary—the only hope—is to bring overwhelming majorities to bear.

So strange, then, that so many people on the left-of-center seem so dedicated to dividing the world up into smaller and smaller constituencies. There's always a way to slice the onion thinner and thinner. You might consider the narrowing of "people of color" to "BIPOC," Black and Indigenous people of color. The purpose of that distinction is to underline the greater oppression that Black and Indigenous Americans have endured than other people of color. And they probably have. The operative question, though, is: What is the political value of dividing progressive constituencies up into smaller and smaller groups? How does that help anyone achieve any of their specific aims, including BIPOC people? Maybe other people of color will better understand the plight of BIPOC people and feel more sympathetic. Or maybe non-BIPOC POC will absorb the lesson that BIPOC people are not like them, not part of their circle or movement or clan, and care less about their plight. This is the danger with insisting that a smaller group is more victimized and thus more deserving of help than another larger group within the progressive coalition; like it or not, for good or bad, most people approach politics by asking, "What's in it for me?" The problem with identity politics is that any given identity is always going to be smaller than the broader possible coalition you could assemble, and almost always smaller than you need to create change.

Lately, it's become the fashion to disdain cisgender white gay men as part of the LGBTQ+ community. They are, apparently, too laden with privilege to be considered part of the coalition of the noble suffering. That sort of thinking is permanently alien to me, so I can't comment on the moral logic at play. But politically it's straightforwardly suicidal; there are millions of cisgender white gay men, they're disproportionately well-connected in politics (yes, thanks to racism and sexism), and they played an outsize role in the fight for gay marriage, one of the most stunningly successful progressive movements in our country's history. Yet, to pick one example, take it from a 2017 piece titled "White Gay Men Are Hindering Our Progress as a Queer Community" by Gabriel Arana, which has the admirably straightforward subhead "You had your time—now, we have other things to fight for." To which I would immediately ask, if that's true, and the LGBTQ+ movement should no longer fight for white gay men, *why would white gay men fight for the LGBTQ+ movement?* If your interest lies in sniping at people on Twitter, then sure, go ahead and chop up the pool of potential supporters for progressive change into smaller and smaller pieces, and tell most people within it that their problems aren't problems. If you want to actually change things, then you need to make sure everyone within your movement is taken seriously and treated well.

Consider police violence—again. As I mentioned in the chapter on Black Lives Matter, annually a majority of people killed by the police are white. During the days of greatest public anger about George Floyd's murder, pointing this fact out came to be seen as wicked and racist; we weren't worrying about white people in that moment, the story went. But white people have a large numerical majority in the United States, an even larger numerical majority among voters, and (as the anti-racist set will tell you) enjoy disproportionate power in our political system. So, what's better messaging: Police violence is a Black people problem that only Black people suffer from, a message that will convince a lot of white people that it's not their problem? Or: Police violence falls especially hard on the Black community, but it hurts all of us, and, in fact, a majority of the victims are white? We need a national reckoning with this problem to stop the violence and save innocent people of all races. It's in the best interest of all of us.

The second is a fundamentally more effective political message, as it avoids defining the problem as a "Black problem." We can still recognize, as a community of the like-minded, that police violence against Black Americans is vastly disproportionate and an expression of racism. We aren't denying that police violence falls especially heavily on Black people. But when we engage in politics, in the work of trying to build the biggest coalition possible for making change, we take care not to pretend that police violence is only a Black problem. We don't moderate or compromise on the actual policies that we demand. We work to build the biggest possible coalition, which always entails—which must entail—appealing to people's sense of self-interest, not to their abstract sense of justice for others. I say that as a big fan of caring about the justice of others.

Is that "fair"? Who cares? If you want change, you have to enlist the help of the powerful. That's life. Do you want to lose pure or win by compromising? Not even compromising on goals, just on messaging! The question answers itself.

TALK LIKE HUMAN BEINGS AGAIN

I'm not a professor, or otherwise officially connected to any academic institution, but I'll always be an academic. I grew up in an academic household, I have a PhD, and I read academic publications regularly. I'll always be an academic at heart.

I say this to ward off any accusations of anti-intellectualism that might follow from what I have to say: The left desperately needs to lose its academic vocabulary. Much of left discourse is incomprehensible to ordinary Americans. Contemporary left discourse has been overwhelmingly influenced by trends in humanities departments at elite universities; students go through those programs and absorb a certain vocabulary, they graduate out and go to work at nonprofits and in media and in Hollywood, and from there they spread the terminology. Social media, especially Tumblr and Twitter, helps ensure that this fancy vocabulary colonizes left-leaning spaces. Nobody wants to sound unsophisticated, so everyone adopts these terms even if they're not particularly comfortable with them. Like seemingly everything in the internet age, it's mimetic. And that's how you get people talking about the role of Latinx intersectionality in queering BIPOC spaces in the global south.

This isn't merely a matter of using esoteric terms either, but of using ordinary language in ways many people find bizarre. Look at the use of the word "bodies," most often heard in relation to Black bodies. At some point in the past half decade or so, it became the fashion in left discursive spaces to speak about Black bodies instead of Black people—this protest was marked by the presence of Black bodies, the white gaze fetishizes Black bodies, academia is inhospitable to Black bodies. . . . If I squint hard enough, I can sort of understand the rationale here; emphasizing bodies emphasizes corporeality, the physical reality of having a body, and in doing so underlines the threat Black people are often under. I could, I suppose, see the utility of saying, "The police's actions put Black bodies in danger." But too often, "Black bodies" is just an awkward and exclusionary euphemism for "people," and a term used to show that someone is a savvy, progressive person with the correct attitudes toward race.

Language is core to persuasion and persuasion is core to politics. Since the left needs to bring people power to bear against the entrenched position of our ruling elite, exclusionary vocabulary can only hurt us. We should always keep an eye toward explaining our values and our policies in simple terms about whom they help and how. This doesn't have to be complicated. In 1948, the British government distributed a pamphlet about its recently implemented national health care system. It began:

YOUR NEW NATIONAL HEALTH SERVICE BEGINS ON 5TH JULY. WHAT IS IT? HOW DO YOU GET IT?

It will provide you with all medical, dental and nursing care. Everyone—rich or poor, man, woman or child—can use it or any part of it. There are no charges, except for a few special items. There are no insurance qualifications. But it is not a "charity." You are all paying for it, mainly as tax payers, and it will relieve your money worries in time of illness.

This is a model of clear language that explains the value of an essential public service, and a demonstration of how the left should talk about its policies.

There's nothing wrong with using an academic term when it actually casts light on your subject, when it makes thinking clearer rather than more complicated. The trouble is that language is so deeply related to belonging—that we often use jargon not to be more understandable or specific but to show that we are a part of a given community, to signal. The thorny complications of contemporary identity politics vocabulary demonstrate why that signaling function can be so fraught. Our guide should always be sense, and we should take care to remember the difference between a conversation between insiders and the kind of talk we want to broadcast to as many people as we can.

As complicated as necessary; as simple as possible.

TELL PEOPLE WHAT YOU HAVE DONE AND WILL DO FOR THEM

Speaking of that NHS pamphlet reminds me that we should also take care to constantly speak plainly about what we have accomplished for our communities. Politics entails clashes of values, and it's not unusual for political argument to become very abstract. But for those of us on the left, our argumentative advantage will almost always lie in relentlessly expressing the social benefits of our beliefs, in telling individual people why their lives are better thanks to our initiatives.

The focus on simply stating the benefits provided by our programs is particularly important for the left for several reasons. One is timeless: it's the left that believes in good government and the capacity for public services to enrich and protect our people, while the right prefers a society that has minimal responsibility to protect its citizens. Conservatives will always harp on taxes and onerous regulations, making a negative argument against the kind of programs and services that progressives advocate for. To do so, they will often slip into debate about abstractions like freedom and fiscal responsibility. Following their lead and dealing in abstractions amounts to playing the game by their rules. If a conservative insists that Social Security taxes are an affront to their liberty, respond by pointing out that the program has lifted millions of senior citizens out of poverty. If a Republican attacks Medicare as an example of government largesse, fight to keep the focus on the millions of Americans who have only gotten chemotherapy and orthopedic surgery thanks to our commitment to ensuring their access to health care. When they talk about a culture of dependency, remind everyone that food stamps are all that stands in the way of millions of kids going hungry. Stay grounded; don't let them push you off the facts of the material benefits of progressive programs.

Another reason for focusing on the simple benefits of progressive programs is timely: the American right has been slipping deeper and deeper into deranged conspiracy theories for years. The specific dimensions of the conspiracy theories change—as I write this, the lunacy of QAnon seems to be finally dying off—but the conspiratorial thinking and willingness to entertain totally bizarre claims never dies. Liberals, leftists, and Democrats would do well by responding with an affirmative argument for the programs we champion. You can't talk a conspiracy theorist out of their theories, and certainly not with logic. Such people are beyond help. While there are times when debunking their nonsense is important, in general you should refuse to play their game. Don't get bogged down in their arguments that, say, elite Democrats traffic, sexually assault, and eat children. You'll just get dragged down to their level if you try to debunk such nonsense. Stay specific and stay positive; provide a more compelling and attractive vision of the America you want to build than they do. Meet Republican lunacy with reminders of what we have done and what we can do.

I PROMISE IT'S OK TO CALL NONSENSE NONSENSE

We live in culture-war hell. The internet ensures that many of us spend all day, every day surrounded by the opinions of people we can't stand. In the scrum of the day-to-day turf war for the American soul, even minor skirmishes can seem to take on world-historical purpose. And in a relentlessly binary political culture, people frequently feel that to give any ground to "the other side" at all is to admit defeat. Which means that progressive culture warriors will often go to the wall for positions they see as broadly on their side, even if they're so extreme as to be ridiculous. They'll throw their full weight behind ideas and statements and arguments that they secretly feel to be stupid, so as not to tacitly lend support to the right.

I promise: you don't have to do that.

For example, there are people who earnestly believe that the phrase "I see what you mean" is ableist—that is, disrespectful and oppressive toward people with disabilities—because some people can't see. This is—and I choose the word carefully—nuts. It's nuts in several different dimensions all at once. Setting aside the unfortunate conflations inherent to the concept of ableism, which aggregates together conditions that have no business being aggregated together, this prohibition insults blind people, pretends to misunderstand the way language works, and is fundamentally unserious. It insults blind people and those with reduced vision because it assumes that they are incredibly sensitive and fragile, that if they come into contact with a perfectly common turn of phrase they've encountered all of their lives, they will be broken by it. As is true of so many contemporary progressive norms, this prohibition belittles and condescends to the very people it ostensibly honors. I have a disability myself, a mental illness. I am not hurt or offended by people using the word "crazy," because I'm not so fragile as that and because I know how language works.

Which leads to the second problem: Metaphorical language is a fact of life. Human beings use terms in figurative senses that diverge from the literal meanings; they always have, they always will. Besides, "I see what you mean" is so abstract that it's barely a metaphor at all. Not to be outdone, some disability activists also nominate "I stand with you" as an ableist saying. Again, this is just how language works—we use more concrete terminology to express abstract ideas. And even if we purged our language of the words "standing" or "seeing," would the paralyzed or the blind somehow forget their conditions and the challenges they face in the world?

Which is the most important point of all: Abstract language games have no real benefit for anyone at all. Blind people, paralyzed people,

people with all manner of mental and physical disabilities—they have real problems navigating the world around them, thanks to human systems that are too often indifferent to their needs. Addressing their problems in concrete ways is politics, and activism. Erasing the phrase "I see what you mean" does nothing for them, nothing at all. Every moment spent trying to police language is a moment not spent on getting a ramp installed at a business or brail installed in an elevator. Such prohibitions have the look and feel of politics, but they are not politics, as nothing so purely abstract ever could be.

Often enough, defenses of this kind of progressive absurdity don't really defend the substance of the issue at hand but rather assert the irrelevance of the conversation. "Sure," they'll say, "it's silly to forbid the phrase 'I see what you mean,' but who cares? That's just something you see on Tumblr; it doesn't matter." The problem with this deflection is that these norms keep moving from the fringes into institutions, where they then spread into the culture. In the early and mid-2010s, I documented a lot of the excesses and mistakes made in the name of social justice on college campuses. I was told, over and over again, that these issues were confined to fancy colleges and thus no big deal. I then watched as those values spread with remarkable efficiency out from the universities and into mainstream left-leaning culture.

And, indeed, as I write this, a minor controversy has erupted of just the kind that I'm talking about here: the University of Southern California's School of Social Work has recently banned the use of the word "field" to refer to an academic discipline, as in "the field of history." This is ostensibly because the word "field" might make Black students and staff think of slavery. What Black person could ever possibly avoid hearing talk about fields, real or metaphorical? When nonsense goes unchallenged because it's perceived to be "on our side," it metastasizes and spreads, until suddenly most left-leaning people feel compelled to defend it. And ordinary people (that is, people not marinating in Twitter every day) will rightfully recognize the absurdity when they see it.

This book is not about "wokeness." I'm not interested in spending a lot of time chewing through social justice language or norms. But I do want to say this: It's OK to call nonsense nonsense, even if you feel it's on your side. I promise. You can defend your values, be a soldier for social justice, and be merciless toward conservatives while still admitting when feckless people take liberal ideology to bizarre ends. It's OK. It's better than OK: we have problems enough without handing conservatives fodder, without gifting them talking points, without alienating ordinary Americans. The social justice movement, for all of its faults, usually points in the right general direction. But I assure you that it's not the first political movement in the history of the world to ever make a mistake. Let other people be good soldiers. You tell the truth, and this includes when progressives are speaking nonsense—again.

THE DEMOCRATIC PARTY: NEITHER EVERYTHING NOR NOTHING

It's a dichotomy I've had to deal with my entire political life: The haughty insistence from the center-left that the only effective political action involves petitioning the Democratic Party, on one side, and the showy dismissal of partisan politics altogether on the other. Both of these perspectives entail a failure of imagination.

Those haughty centrists will tell you that there is no positive progressive action that does not fall under the auspices of the Democratic Party; correspondingly, there's no such thing as appropriate criticism of the Democratic Party, as any such criticism must inevitably lend support to the Republican Party. This attitude fails to understand the full sweep of what political action entails and the various battlegrounds on which the war for progress is fought. There are, in fact, types of action that have real-world political consequence that don't take place within the confines of establishment politics. I've already mentioned the potential for strike actions to achieve positive change outside of the typical political process; other groups, such as those dedicated to environmentalism, have effectively used the courts to pursue their agendas without the blessings of the Democrats. And while protests have goals that are typically more diffuse and less mechanistic, they can raise awareness in a way that leads to eventual change. The anti–Vietnam War movement, for example, was largely antagonistic to the Democratic Party, and it helped make Lyndon Johnson's reputation so toxic that he declined to run for reelection in 1968.

For their own part, those Marxists I've known who dismiss any of the results of partisan politics as a shuffling of the representatives of the ruling class are ceding the field of a core means of changing the world. That neither partisan alternative is particularly appealing in our political system neither means that the differences don't matter nor that it makes sense to abandon that approach to change-making. As annoying as they may be, partisan Democrats are correct in pointing out that the outcomes of elections have immense consequences for issues of basic justice in our society. Electoral politics is an instrument of power; wiping your hands of it disempowers you.

I look on my six-plus years working in the tenants' rights movement in New York City as a good example of how partisan politics can be balanced with tactics and techniques from outside of that system. There are myriad organizations that participate in the movement, some that are very cozy with the local Democratic Party, some that keep partisan politics at arm's length. Some of the actions these groups undertake are decidedly outside of politics as usual, such as organizations that find emergency housing for evicted tenants or that publicly shame landlords until they make necessary repairs. Some are simply lobbying, asking

Democrats in Albany and city hall to pass laws or use their position to pressure city agencies into taking action. And sometimes, the movement's work is essentially hybrid—my own organization runs a hotline where we provide direct advice to tenants, but that advice is about the interpretation of laws and regulations that are subject to the influence of partisan politics. One of the movement's biggest victories was the passage of the 2019 Housing Safety and Tenant Protection Act, but getting that bill passed through the system took years of tenant organizing to create the pressure points that eventually made partisan political gain possible. Influencing Democrats is an important part of the tenant movement in New York, but without dedicated organizing in other venues, the movement would not be what it is.

Democrats dismissive of activism and radicals who disdain partisan politics are both guilty of the same sin, putting an emotional relationship to the Democrats before strategic best interest—the partisan Democrats, of being too emotionally invested in the party; the radicals, of letting their disdain for the Democrats close their minds to the possibilities of the partisan political arena.

If you're left-of-center, the Democrats will disappoint you. That's what they do; they're the Democrats. But what happens in the political arena is simply too important to wash your hands of them. For better or worse, we have to find the pressure points to influence the Democrats to line up with our values. We have to press them.

STOP WAITING FOR THE REVOLUTION OF THE YOUTH

The left has always romanticized youth. Young people are viewed as the hope for a more progressive future, reflexively and unthinkingly and to the degree that this is not really thought of as a prediction about the future at all but more as a fact of the universe. Indeed, I find that a lot of lefties become very defensive if you question whether we can, in fact, trust the youth to come and save us. It's my experience that a lot of people praise the youth and disdain the elderly because they want to feel young too.

And yet we have a repetitive history to remind us that the youth, no matter how radical they may be, don't create permanent positive change. The hippies of the 1960s became the yuppies of the 1980s. The radical labor movements of the 1910s became, in time, the conservative unions of the mid twentieth century. Now regularly dismissed as an apathetic generation, in the 1990s, Gen X was thought of as a radical group, developing political correctness as a mass vocabulary and bringing the 1999 World Trade Organization meetings to a halt with the Battle for Seattle protests. What came next was the post-9/11 period with its retrenchment into paranoid nationalism and xenophobia. My own generation, the Millennials, has been regarded as the radical generation many times, with the argument being that because we have suffered economically compared to earlier generations we would inevitably push for progressive economic policies. We're now mostly in our thirties and forties; we don't appear to be in an era of left-wing triumph. I don't think any of these generations "failed." I think that, like any, they were immensely more complex and internally conflicted than broad generalizations allowed, and I think that politics is cyclical; progressive foment leads to conservative retrenchment leads to another new dawn. That's the way of things.

Whether people actually get more conservative as they age, or whether older cohorts are simply more conservative than younger, is a matter of dispute. But we need to distinguish self-professed conservatism from structural self-interest here—the former is when you believe in right-wing ideology and will both advocate for it and let it guide your voting behavior; the latter is when your position in society compels you to advocate for public policy that is de facto conservative. A classic example is the behavior of homeowners, who will typically do whatever they can to protect the value of their homes, as for most of them, their houses represent a significant majority of their net worth. They will therefore frequently fight to prevent new construction such as subsidized housing in their neighborhoods. Famously, homeowners will often act this way even though they hold explicitly progressive politics, the kind of politics that would ordinarily lead them to support subsidized housing. This general principle holds in all manner of political affairs: Once people have a little money and a little property and a desire to protect them, their political behavior will often become self-interested and thus conservative even if they maintain left-wing ideals. This can be part of why radical young generations so often fail to produce enduring radical change; they become preoccupied with protecting what they already have.

Besides—suppose it is true that the youth of today are and will remain significantly to the left of past generations. Would the axis of right and left cease to function? We would still be stuck in the scrum of left and right, the day-to-day push and pull of opposing interests and people who want society to move a little more right or a little more left. I'm not saying any of this to suggest that progress is impossible or that our political world is static; indeed, it's ever-changing. I'm pointing out that the idea of a final victory, brought by a radical young generation, is based on the faulty belief that the work will ever stop. Every new generation will be replaced by another new generation, and they'll find something to fight about. The work of politics will always grind on.

Should we have a more authentically left-wing future, the Republicans will adapt; they will moderate on some issues, double down on others, and they will win and lose elections as they win and lose elections now. And the potential for retrenchment is written into human history, even into recent American history. The story of human society is the story of a series of tightenings and loosenings of social mores. The freewheeling 1920s gave way in time to the stultifying morals of the 1940s and '50s. The radical ferment of the 1960s, predicted in real time to change the world, was followed in time by the Reaganite 1980s. Things change. Sometimes this change is good, sometimes it's bad, and sometimes you get to choose which it is.

The future will not be liberal or conservative, neither left wing nor right. It will just be different.

NO ONE IS COMING TO SAVE US

The young aren't coming to save us. And neither is anyone else.

People like to imagine the means of their deliverance. Dreams of a utopian future where everything is different crowd our collective head-space. Sometimes it feels like everyone has become a millenarian. As I write this, it's become fashionable to talk about an artificial intelligence revolution, one that will bring abundance, "disrupting" countless industries and eliminating waste—and, perhaps, destroying the labor market, costing millions their jobs. You see, people also spend a lot of time thinking about the apocalypse, about the end times; the postapocalyptic tale is a hoary old genre, filled with commonplaces and clichés. There seems to be an insatiable desire for something like an *end*, an end to the good and the bad, a transition to a wholly different future where today's quotidian problems are gone. No one has more of an attachment to both utopian and apocalyptic scenarios than the radical left, which imagines the triumphal revolution and the fascist takeover with equal fervor. These are seemingly opposite instincts, and yet they share the same underlying desire: to be rescued from the ordinary. To be freed from the grubby constraints of the same old arguments, the same old patterns.

I get it. I used to be the same way, yawing constantly between believing that utopia was now and that the end was near. The dispiriting reality around me seemed unbearable, and I yearned for its end. One way or another.

In time, I had to grow out of this affectation. I had to come to terms with the fact that the only true radicalism is one that's willing to exist in the world as it is, one that never ceases trying to change the system but refuses to give in to the temptation of trying to escape it. The only deliverance is the one we make.

This is what I want to tell you, more than anything: You cannot wait for something or someone to come and save us. You cannot count on an end to the dull grind of daily politics. The foment of 2020 was transformative to many people, and for many reasons. But the simplest one was the palpable feeling—*this time is different.* You'd go out to the BLM protests, feel the energy, hear the slogans, see the righteous rage, and feel like something had to give. For a brief moment, it felt like the glass was breaking. And then time went on, and nothing much changed, and it turned out that the well-worn grooves of contemporary politics are hard to get out of. And what I would like most to convince young leftists of is to stop expecting politics to fundamentally and dramatically change. To stop waiting for the revolution. I am trying, in other words, to *rehabilitate the ordinary* in far-left American politics.

Or, as I often put it—they're not just going to stop making Republicans. Movement conservatism will not just dry up and blow away. No one alive will live to see the end of fascism. The forces of reaction will be with us always. And they too will have their say.

This will, naturally, be viewed as an endorsement of incrementalism, of business as usual, as a denial of the possibility of revolution, of centrism. But that perspective is incorrect. I believe in the possibility of transformative change in my own lifetime. True single-payer health insurance in the United States, typically called Medicare for All, appears like a distant dream. The private health insurance industry naturally opposes it, as if it was passed it would mean the end of private insurance. (It is possible that we could pass single-payer and the health insurance industry would hang around, acting as an intermediary between the government and the people getting health care, as it does with Medicare today; this would be a depressing but profoundly American turn of events.) Though some polling shows broad support for single-payer, this support is susceptible to the wording of poll questions, and Americans are also resistant to the end of private insurance. (Such incoherence is not unusual in public polling.)

But things change, and sometimes they change quickly. Gay marriage is a fundamentally different issue than single-payer health care—in particular, because gay marriage did not threaten an immense private industry the way single-payer does—but it's still worth considering just what a remarkable transformation was seen in this country regarding that issue. In 2004, Republican strategist Karl Rove used gay marriage as a wedge issue, utilizing it to bludgeon John Kerry in his failed campaign to replace George W. Bush in the White House. Not twenty years later, even most Republicans don't attempt to run against gay marriage in elections, because that right seems so deeply established now. (And, as of 2022, it is enshrined in federal law, rather than merely required by Supreme Court precedent.) For most of our country's history, that marriage was between a man and a woman was so deeply ingrained an idea that it wasn't seen as a political question at all. In 1996, a Democratic president signed the Defense of Marriage Act, which banned gay marriage, and he bragged about it. Then, a small minority of passionate people had a vision for something different, worked both within and outside of the partisan political system, and changed the country. Something like that could happen with health care too.

But—if single-payer were passed tomorrow, then we would have to start defending it tomorrow. We'd have to fight over how generous the benefits were. We would have to ensure that dental and vision benefits were covered. We would have to prevent the inevitable attempts by conservatives to tear down the system entirely or to make it considerably less generous, as they already do with Medicare and Social Security. After one of the greatest left-wing victories that seems remotely plausible in contemporary American life, we would immediately begin the next fight. There would be no rest.

This is, I concede, a depressing condition, an exhausting one. But there's no alternative. And perhaps there shouldn't be. I still yearn for revolution, but I now recognize that any revolution must be a permanent one, in the sense meant by Karl Marx and Friedrich Engels—that a perpetual revolutionary class must exist, remaining independent from the political machinery of its day and constantly pressing for a more radical future, even after great victory. This is the only way to truly secure the best good for the most people, by seeing political success as an ever-receding horizon. Never forget that there is always work that you can do. Your work will rarely feel as momentous as when millions took to the streets in 2020. But the steady and unromantic work of making the world a little better, one day at a time, has its own rewards. Wherever you are, there are likely organizations whose work is consonant with your values. Research them. Go to a meeting. See if they're the kind of people you would be happy to work with. Then picket, or protest, or persuade, or stuff envelopes, or hand out leaflets, or bug your state legislator, or hold a sign by the side of the highway, or organize a tenants' association, or raise money, or boycott, or what you will. You will not be able to see the change you make. But you will feel it anyway.

We're fighting today; we'll fight tomorrow. Sometimes we'll win more and sometimes we'll win less, and always the work will grind on.

And, every once in a while, we'll celebrate.

ACKNOWLEDGMENTS

I would like to thank William Callahan and InkWell Management, Robert Messenger and Simon & Schuster, and Hamish McKenzie and the rest of the team at Substack. I would like to thank my family—Anika, John, Aurora, Hendrik, Kerste, and Aeris. I would like to thank Met Council on Housing for giving me the tools to help others. I would like to thank Brooklyn College for firing me and in doing so setting me free. I would like to thank my cat, Suavecito, for never changing. And, most important, I would like to thank 은혜, who is my present, my future, and my purpose.

NOTES

1: WHATEVER HAPPENED TO 2020?

16   **Notoriously, only one senior banker:** Jesse Eisinger, "Why Only One Top Banker Went to Jail for the Financial Crisis," *New York Times*, April 30, 2014, https://www.nytimes.com/2014/05/04/magazine/only-one-top -banker-jail-financial-crisis.html.

17   **"Obama, in fact, was the conservative":** Andrew Sullivan, "The Triumph of Obama's Long Game," *New York*, July 21, 2017, https://nymag.com /intelligencer/2017/07/the-triumph-of-obamas-long-game.html.

17   **"Barack Obama ran for and entered":** Perry Bacon Jr., "Hope and Change? Obama's Legacy at a Crossroads," *NBC News*, December 26, 2016.

19   **"Protesters Debate What Demands":** Meredith Hoffman, "Protesters Debate What Demands, if Any, to Make," *New York Times*, October 16, 2011, https://www.nytimes.com/2011/10/17/nyregion/occupy-wall-street -trying-to-settle-on-demands.html.

22   **"Contrary to what we would like":** Jo Freeman, "The Tyranny of Structurelessness," JoFreeman.com, https://www.jofreeman.com/joreen/tyranny .htm.

26   **though American taxes were not:** "History of Federal Income Tax Rates: 1913–2023," Bradford Tax Institute, https://bradfordtaxinstitute.com/free _resources/federal-income-tax-rates.aspx.

26   **True or not, the Tea Party:** Karlyn Bowman and Jennifer Marsico, "As the Tea Party Turns Five, It Looks a Lot Like the Conservative Base," *Forbes*, February 24, 2014, https://www.forbes.com/sites/realspin/2014/02/24 /as-the-tea-party-turns-five-it-looks-a-lot-like-the-conservative-base/? sh=31a495e4f0cc.

27 **It's also true that she:** Chris Cillizza, "4 Theories on Why Hillary Clinton Isn't Very Popular Right Now," CNN.com, January 5, 2018, https://www .cnn.com/2017/12/20/politics/hillary-clinton-bill-clinton-poll-analysis /index.html.

29 **The organization tripled in membership size:** Matt Pearce, "Seeing Red: Membership Triples for the Democratic Socialists of America," *Los Angeles Times*, March 12, 2017, https://www.latimes.com/nation/la-na-democrat ic-socialists-20170308-story.html.

33 **It was estimated that:** Larry Buchanan, Quoctrung Bui, and Jugal K. Patel, "Black Lives Matter May Be the Largest Movement in U.S. History," *New York Times*, July 3, 2020, https://www.nytimes.com/interactive/2020/07/03 /us/george-floyd-protests-crowd-size.html.

34 **"it is an error to jump":** Jonathan Chait, "The Still-Vital Case for Liberalism in a Radical Age," *New York*, June 11, 2020, https://nymag.com /intelligencer/2020/06/case-for-liberalism-tom-cotton-new-york-times -james-bennet.html.

36 **"For years, I've been among":** Wesley Lowery, "A Reckoning Over Objectivity, Led by Black Journalists," *New York Times*, June 23, 2020, https:// www.nytimes.com/2020/06/23/opinion/objectivity-black-journalists-coro navirus.html.

37 **Take, for example, the fact:** Ian Thomsen, "The Research Is Clear: White People Are Not More Likely Than Black People to Be Killed by Police," *Northeastern Global News*, July 16, 2020, https://news.northeastern .edu/2020/07/16/the-research-is-clear-white-people-are-not-more-like ly-than-black-people-to-be-killed-by-police/.

37 **"The killing of Trayvon Martin":** Mansfield Frazier, "After Trayvon, Conservatives Discover Black-on-Black Violence," *Daily Beast*, April 9, 2012, https://www.thedailybeast.com/after-trayvon-conservatives-discover -black-on-black-violence.

38 **"Yes, We Mean Literally Abolish":** Mariame Kaba, "Yes, We Mean Literally Abolish the Police," *New York Times*, June 12, 2020, https://www.nytimes .com/2020/06/12/opinion/sunday/floyd-abolish-defund-police.html.

40 **No doubt influenced by the country's:** Sasha Pezenik, "2020 Democratic Candidates Move to the Left, Become More Progressive as Climate Change Emerges as Campaign Issue," *ABC News*, June 7, 2019, https://abcnews .go.com/Politics/2020-democratic-candidates-move-left-progressive -climate-change/story?id=63489543.

40 **"may make it difficult for":** Jonathan Martin and Alexander Burns,

"Bernie Sanders Wins Nevada Caucuses, Strengthening His Primary Lead,"
New York Times, February 22, 2020, https://www.nytimes.com/2020/02/22
/us/politics/bernie-sanders-nevada-caucus.html.

41　**It was widely reported:** Carol E. Lee, Kristen Welker, Josh Lederman,
and Amanda Golden, "Looking for Obama's Hidden Hand in Candidates
Coalescing around Biden," *NBC News,* March 2, 2020, https://www.nbc
news.com/politics/2020-election/looking-obama-s-hidden-hand-candi
date-coalescing-around-biden-n1147471.

2: BPMCLM: BLACK LIVES MATTER AND THE INEVITABILITY OF ELITE CAPTURE

47　**The average white American:** Ember Smith, Ariel Gelrud Shiro, Chris-
topher Pulliam, and Richard V. Reeves, "The Black-White Gap in Wealth
Mobility and What to Do about It," Brookings Institute, June 29, 2020,
https://www.brookings.edu/blog/up-front/2022/06/29/the-black-white
-gap-in-wealth-mobility-and-what-to-do-about-it/.

47　**In December 2022, 3 percent:** "Civilian Unemployment Rate," US Bureau
of Labor Statistics, https://www.bls.gov/charts/employment-situation
/civilian-unemployment-rate.htm.

47　**The poverty rate of white Americans:** "Poverty Rate by Race/Ethnicity,"
Kaiser Family Foundation, 2021, https://www.kff.org/2d5cbf8/.

47　**62.5 percent of white Americans:** Imed Bouchrika, "Number of College Graduates: 2023 Race, Gender, Age & State Statistics," Universities
& Colleges, Research.com, September 29, 2022, https://research.com
/universities-colleges/number-of-college-graduates.

47　**In 2019, the average life span:** National Institutes of Health, "Life Expec-
tancy in the U.S. Increased between 2000–2019, but Widespread Gaps
Among Racial and Ethnic Groups Exist," US Department of Health &
Human Services, June 16, 2022, https://www.nih.gov/news-events/news
-releases/life-expectancy-us-increased-between-2000-2019-widespread
-gaps-among-racial-ethnic-groups-exist.

47　**In 2019, 73.3 percent of white:** "Homeownership Rates Show that Black
Americans Are Currently the Least Likely Group to Own Homes,"
USAFacts, July 28, 2020.

48　**In 2021, the rate of imprisonment:** Adriana Rezal, "The Racial Makeup
of America's Prisons," *U.S. News & World Report*, October 13, 2021, https://
www.usnews.com/news/best-states/articles/2021-10-13/report-high
lights-staggering-racial-disparities-in-us-incarceration-rates.

48　**In 2020, 6.2 percent:** Chris Uggen, Ryan Larson, Sarah Shannon, and

Arleth Pulido-Nava, "Locked Out 2020: Estimates of People Denied Voting Rights Due to a Felony Conviction," Sentencing Project, October 30, 2020, https://www.sentencingproject.org/reports/locked-out-2020-estimates-of -people-denied-voting-rights-due-to-a-felony-conviction/.

48 **According to the *Washington Post*, 1,096 people:** "Fatal Force," *Washington Post*, accessed January 11, 2023, https://www.washingtonpost.com/graphics /investigations/police-shootings-database/.

50 **According to the Equal Justice Initiative:** "Qualified Immunity," Equal Justice Initiative, accessed January 26, 2023.

52 **A YouGov poll conducted:** Linley Sanders, "What Police Reform Does America Support?," YouGovAmerica, June 1, 2020, https://today.yougov .com/topics/politics/articles-reports/2020/06/01/police-reform-america -poll.

52 **Some Democrats representing liberal:** David Winston, "'Defund the Police' Still Haunts Democrats," *Roll Call*, April 27, 2022, https://rollcall .com/2022/04/27/defund-the-police-still-haunts-democrats/.

53 **It was therefore somewhat useful:** Kaba, "Yes, We Mean Literally Abolish the Police."

56 **Those charges were eventually dropped:** Jonah E. Bromwich, "Amy Cooper, Who Falsely Accused Black Bird-Watcher, Has Charge Dismissed," *New York Times*, February 16, 2021, https://www.nytimes.com/2021/02/16 /nyregion/amy-cooper-charges-dismissed.html?smid=url-share.

57 **There were no doubt millions:** "Fatal Force," *Washington Post*.

57 **"Pew Research Center, for example,":** Kim Parker and Kiley Hurst, "Growing Share of Americans Say They Want More Spending on Police in Their Area," Pew Research Center, October 26, 2021, https://www.pewresearch .org/fact-tank/2021/10/26/growing-share-of-americans-say-they-want -more-spending-on-police-in-their-area/.

57 **Similarly, a Gallup poll from:** Lydia Saad, "Black Americans Want Police to Retain Local Presence," Gallup, August 5, 2020, https://news.gallup.com /poll/316571/black-americans-police-retain-local-presence.aspx.

58 **An October 2022 poll of Black:** Gerren Keith Gaynor, "Most Black Voters Tell the theGrio/KFF Survey They Support Funding or Increased Funding for Police," TheGrio/KFF, October 25, 2022, https://thegrio.com/2022/10/25 /black-voters-thegrio-kff-funding-police/.

58 **A June 2022 poll:** Chris Simkins, "Poll Finds Most Americans Support US Police Reforms," VOA, June 2, 2022, https://www.voanews.com/a /poll-finds-most-americans-support-us-police-reforms/6600984.html.

58 **"on a number of racial issues":** Daniel A. Cox, "Crime, Policing, and the Racial Divide on the Left," Survey Center on American Life, February 22, 2022, https://www.americansurveycenter.org/crime-policing-and-the -racial-divide-on-the-left/.

59 **A 2020 paper from:** Aaron Chalfin, Benjamin Hansen, Emily K. Weisburst, and Morgan C. Williams Jr., "Police Force Size and Civilian Race," *American Economic Review: Insights* 4, no. 2 (December 2022): 139–58.

60 **"Community Justice works":** Community Justice Action Fund, https:// www.cjactionfund.org/, accessed March 6, 2023.

61 **"In 2020 those identifying":** Justin Fox, "Homicide Is Pandemic's Biggest Killer of Young Black Men," *Washington Post*, February 23, 2022.

63 **"a conflict over how":** Liam Kofi Bright, "White Psychodrama," *Journal of Political Philosophy*, preprint, submitted November 5, 2021.

64 **"In 2019, about four in ten Black":** Amina Dunn, "5 Facts About Black Democrats," Pew Research Center, February 27, 2020, https://www.pew research.org/fact-tank/2020/02/27/5-facts-about-black-democrats/.

66 **In 1940, Black high school:** Jennifer Cheeseman Day, "Black High School Attainment Nearly on Par with National Average," United States Census Bureau, June 10, 2020, https://www.census.gov/library/stories/2020/06 /black-high-school-attainment-nearly-on-par-with-national-average.html.

66 **For one example, from 2018:** Jonathan Dunn, Sheldon Lyn, Nony Onyeador, and Ammanuel Zegeye, "Black Representation in Film and TV: The Challenges and Impact of Increasing Diversity," McKinsey & Company, March 11, 2021, https://www.mckinsey.com/featured-insights /diversity-and-inclusion/black-representation-in-film-and-tv-the-chal lenges-and-impact-of-increasing-diversity.

67 **"We demand that teachers stop":** Conference on College Composition and Communication, "This Ain't Another Statement! This Is a DEMAND for Black Linguistic Justice!," National Council of Teachers of English, July 2020, https://cccc.ncte.org/cccc/demand-for-black-linguistic-justice.

67 **"this global solidarity [which] undoubtedly":** Olúfẹ́mi O. Táíwò, *Elite Capture: How the Powerful Took Over Identity Politics (and Everything Else)* (Chicago: Haymarket Books, 2022), 3.

68 **"At the start of the show":** Eric Deggans, "Jenny Slate and Kristen Bell Will Stop Playing Biracial Cartoon Characters," NPR, June 25, 2020, https://www.npr.org/sections/live-updates-protests-for-racial-justice /2020/06/25/883622069/.

69 **"the Left needs a vocabulary":** Stephen D'Arcy, "The Rise of the Post–New

Left Political Vocabulary," Public Autonomy Project, January 27, 2014, https://publicautonomy.org/2014/01/27/the-rise-of-the-post-new-left-political-vocabulary/.

70   **"Negroes have benefited from"**: Martin Luther King Jr., "MLK's Forgotten Call for Economic Justice," *The Nation*, March 14, 1966, https://www.thenation.com/article/economy/last-steep-ascent/.

70   **"How then have the PoC intelligentsia"**: Bright, "White Psychodrama."

70   **According to the *Washington Post***: Tracy Jan, Jena McGregor, and Meghan Hoyer, "Corporate America's $50 Billion Promise," *Washington Post*, August 23, 2021, https://www.washingtonpost.com/business/interactive/2021/george-floyd-corporate-america-racial-justice/?itid=lk_inline_manual_55.

70   *"Individual donors and independent philanthropic"*: Ann Brown, "$10.6B+ Was Given to Black Lives Matter Causes: Where Did the Money Go?," *Moguldom Nation*, December 16, 2020, https://moguldom.com/323339/10-6b-was-given-to-black-lives-matter-causes-where-did-the-money-go/.

71   **A January 2022 investigation by *New York***: Sean Campbell, "The BLM Mystery: Where Did the Money Go?" *New York*, January 31, 2022, https://nymag.com/intelligencer/2022/01/black-lives-matter-finances.html.

71   **the same reporter later discovered**: Sean Campbell, "Black Lives Matter Secretly Bought a $6 Million House," *New York*, April 4, 2022, https://nymag.com/intelligencer/2022/04/black-lives-matter-6-million-dollar-house.html?utm_campaign=nym&utm_medium=s1&utm_source=tw.

72   **"This idea that we"**: Molly Fischer, "Guilty Parties," *New York*, May 27, 2021, https://www.thecut.com/2021/05/eavesdropping-on-race2dinners-anti-racist-dinner-parties.html#_ga=2.225509210.1751782266.1677644467-2029636008.1677217528.

3: MY PROTEST, YOUR RIOT

81   **"In more than 93% of all"**: "Demonstrations and Political Violence in America: New Data for Summer 2020," ACLED, September 3, 2020.

81   **The left being the left**: Lizzy Acker, "Iconic Portland Elk Statue Removed from Downtown after Fire Set During Protest," *Oregonian*, July 2, 2020, https://www.oregonlive.com/portland/2020/07/iconic-portland-elk-statue-removed-from-downtown-after-fire-set-during-protest.html.

82   **The political news outlet *Axios***: Jennifer A. Kingson, "Exclusive: $1 Billion-Plus Riot Damage Is Most Expensive in Insurance History,"

Axios, September 16, 2020, https://www.axios.com/2020/09/16/riots-cost
-property-damage.

83 **"people what they need for free"**: Natalie Escobar, "One Author's Controversial View: 'In Defense of Looting,'" NPR, August 27, 2020, https://
www.npr.org/sections/codeswitch/2020/08/27/906642178/one-authors
-argument-in-defense-of-looting.

83 **"too many lines have been crossed"**: R. H. Lossin, "In Defense of Destroying Property," *The Nation*, June 10, 2020, https://www.thenation.com
/article/activism/blm-looting-protest-vandalism/.

84 **"only one thing is clear"**: Kellie Carter Jackson, "The Double Standard
of the American Riot," *The Atlantic*, June 1, 2020, https://www.theatlantic
.com/culture/archive/2020/06/riots-are-american-way-george-floyd-pro
tests/612466/.

84 **"suggest a new phase of opposition"**: Thomas J. Sugrue, "2020 Is Not 1968:
To Understand Today's Protests, You Must Look Further Back," *National
Geographic*, June 11, 2020, https://www.nationalgeographic.com/history
/article/2020-not-1968.

84 **"civil disobedience is frenzied"**: Terry Nguyen, "There Isn't a Simple Story about Looting," *Vox*, June 2, 2020, https://www.vox.com/the
-goods/2020/6/2/21278113/looting-george-floyd-protests-social-unrest.

84 **"our country was built on looting"**: Robin D. G. Kelley, "What Kind
of Society Values Property Over Black Lives?," *New York Times*, June 18,
2020, https://www.nytimes.com/2020/06/18/opinion/george-floyd-protests
-looting.html.

84 **"have given the Second Amendment"**: Glenn Harlan Reynolds, "Riots
of 2020 Have Given the Second Amendment a Boost," *USA Today*, October 8, 2020, https://www.usatoday.com/story/opinion/2020/10/08/riots
-2020-have-given-boost-second-amendment-column/5901798002/.

85 **"The limitation of riots"**: Martin Luther King, "A New Sense of Direction
(1968)," Carnegie Council for Ethics in Environmental Affairs, April 30,
1970, https://www.carnegiecouncil.org/media/article/a-new-sense-of
-direction-1968.

94 **In a 2022 poll, only:** Garen J. Wintemute et al., "Views of American
Democracy and Society and Support for Political Violence: First Report
from a Nationwide Population-Representative Survey," Medrxiv, July 19,
2022, https://www.medrxiv.org/content/10.1101/2022.07.15.22277693v1.

94 **Another poll from Reuters/Ipsos:** Ipsos, "Core Political Presidential

Approval Tracker and Biden's Speech on Democracy," Reuters/Ipsos, September 2022, https://www.ipsos.com/sites/default/files/ct/news /documents/2022-09/Ipsos%20Poll%20Presidential%20Approval%20 Tracker%20and%20Biden%27s%20Speech%2009%2008%202022.pdf.

94 **And the polling analysis site:** Kaleigh Rogers and Zoha Qamar, "What Americans Think About Political Violence," FiveThirtyEight, November 4, 2022, https://fivethirtyeight.com/features/what-americans-think-about -political-violence/.

94 **On the subject of the Black Lives Matter:** National Police Association, "Most Voters Want Congress to Investigate the 574 Violent Riots in 2020 that Resulted in Over 2,000 Injured Police Officers as Well as the January 6th Riot at the US Capitol," PR Newswire, July 21, 2021, https://www.prnews wire.com/news-releases/most-voters-want-congress-to-investigate-the-574 -violent-riots-in-2020-that-resulted-in-over-2-000-injured-police-officers -as-well-as-the-january-6th-riot-at-the-us-capitol-301338240.html.

94 **But a similar 2020 poll:** Ipsos, "Civil Unrest in the Wake of George Floyd's Killing," Reuters/Ipsos, June 2, 2020, https://www.ipsos.com/en-us /news-polls/reuters-ipsos-civil-unrest-george-floyd-2020-06-02.

4: THE NONPROFIT INDUSTRIAL COMPLEX

97 **According to the Urban Institute's:** NCCS Project Team, "The Non-profit Sector in Brief 2019," Urban Institute National Center for Charitable Statistics, June 4, 2020, https://nccs.urban.org/publication/nonprofit -sector-brief-2019.

97 **For contrast, according to:** National Center for Education Statistics, "Education Expenditures by Country," *Condition of Education*, US Department of Education, Institute of Education Sciences, May 2022, https://nces.ed .gov/programs/coe/indicator/cmd/education-expenditures-by-country.

97 **According to the National Council of Nonprofits:** "What is a 'Non-profit'?," National Council of Nonprofits, https://www.councilofnonprofits .org/what-is-a-nonprofit.

98 **Between 2007 and 2016:** Chelsea Newhouse, "Nonprofit Rate of Job Growth Outpaces For-Profit Rate by Over 3-1 Over Last Decade," Center for Civil Society Studies Archive, August 28, 2018, http://ccss.jhu.edu /news-release-2016-us-data/.

98 **"Charitable nonprofits embody":** Nonprofit Impact in Communities," National Council of Nonprofits, accessed November 18, 2022, https://www .councilofnonprofits.org/nonprofit-impact-communities.

99 **A 2021 study found:** Elizabeth Bell, Alisa Hicklin Fryar, and Tyler Johnson, "Exploring Public Perceptions of Nonprofit Policy Advocacy," *Nonprofit Policy Forum*, 12, no. 2 (July 2021): 311–40.

99 **It cited a 2009 paper:** Michael O'Neill, "Public Confidence in Charitable Nonprofits," *Nonprofit and Voluntary Sector Quarterly* 38, no. 2 (April 2009): 237–69.

99 **"America's charitable nonprofits rely":** "Ethics & Accountability," National Council of Nonprofits, https://www.councilofnonprofits.org /tools-resources-categories/ethics-accountability.

100 **"Such preferences [for confidentiality]":** Barry D. Friedman and Amanda M. Wolcott, "Transparency in Nonprofit Organizations: Public Access to Minutes of Board Meetings," faculty.ung.edu, October 2, 2015, http:// faculty.ung.edu/bfriedman/Studies/TransMin.html.

100 **"The role of nonprofits":** Alina Clough, "Activism Needs Transparency, Too," *Fulcrum*, August 4, 2022, https://thefulcrum.us/Justice/Accountabil ity/transparency-in-nonprofit-organizations.

101 **"Countless leaders of nonprofit organizations":** Barry D. Friedman and Amanda M. Wolcott. "Secrecy and Transparency in Nonprofit Organizations: If a Nonprofit Prefers Secrecy, What Does It Want to Hide?," Paper for Presentation at the Southeastern Conference on Public Administration, September 21, 2018, https://core.ac.uk/download/pdf/228457672.pdf.

101 **The watchdog organization Charity Navigator:** Robert F. Hart Jr., "What Does Your Program Efficiency Ratio Reveal About Your Nonprofit?," LGA CPAs and Business Advisors, April 9, 2021, https://www.lga.cpa/resources /program-efficiency-ration-reveals-about-nonprofit/.

102 **"It's a badly kept secret":** William Bedsworth, Ann Goggins Gregory, and Don Howard, "Nonprofit Overhead Costs: Breaking the Vicious Cycle of Misleading Reporting, Unrealistic Expectations, and Pressure to Conform," Bridgespan Group, April 1, 2008, https://www.bridgespan.org/insights /nonprofit-overhead-costs-break-the-vicious-cycle.

102 **The American Red Cross:** Anna Staver, "Fact Check: Does Red Cross Really Spend Only 9% of Its Money on Charity?," *Columbus Dispatch*, July 12, 2020, https://www.dispatch.com/story/news/politics/2020/07/13 /fact-check-does-red-cross-really-spend-only-9-of-its-money-on-charity /112175424/.

102 **"GiveWell started when a group":** "About GiveWell," GiveWell, https:// www.givewell.org/about.

103 **"At the end of the day":** Tracy Ebarb, "Nonprofits Fail—Here's Seven

Reasons Why," NANOE, September 7, 2019, https://nanoe.org/nonprof
its-fail/?gclid=Cj0KCQiA6fafBhC1ARIsAIJjL8kOpPXup0SGdu26fr69N
LFfLWxBn9z6GA039wpRwvznfGBm0aGmOBQaAgmDEALw_wcB.

104 **"the people who control institutions":** Jon Schwarz, "Democrats and the
Iron Law of Institutions," *A Tiny Revolution*, September 5, 2007, http://
www.tinyrevolution.com/mt/archives/001705.html.

106 **"The purpose of the nonprofit":** Common Dreams, "A Brutal Concen-
tration of Wealth: How Nonprofits Perpetuate the Dysfunctions of Capitalism," *Milwaukee Independent*, December 22, 2020, http://www.mil
waukeeindependent.com/syndicated/brutal-concentration-wealth-non
profits-perpetuate-dysfunctions-capitalism/.

106 **"There isn't just a lack of ":** Sevetri Wilson, "How to Address Diversity
and Inclusion Issues within the Nonprofit Sector," *Forbes*, October 15,
2020, https://www.forbes.com/sites/forbesbusinesscouncil/2020/10/15
/how-to-address-diversity-and-inclusion-issues-within-the-nonprofit
-sector/?sh=5ffd536d712e.

106 **A 2017 survey from the firm:** "The State of Diversity in Nonprofit and
Foundation Leadership," Battalia Wintson, October 2014. https://www.bat
taliawinston.com/2017/06/07/the-diversity-gap-in-the-nonprofit-sector/.

107 **In 2019, for example:** Kimberley A. Strassel, "The Left's Lucrative Nonprofits," *Wall Street Journal*, September 5, 2019, https://www.wsj.com
/articles/the-lefts-lucrative-nonprofits-11567723794.

107 **"Left-wing activism pays very well":** J. D. Vance, "Stop Treating Left-Wing
Advocacy Groups Like Charities," *Newsweek*, October 13, 2021, https://
www.newsweek.com/stop-treating-left-wing-advocacy-groups-like-char
ities-opinion-1637733.

108 **For example, a *Fast Company*:** Ben Paynter, "Is Silicon Valley's Giant
Foundation Just Hoarding Money?," *Fast Company*, August 7, 2018, https://
www.fastcompany.com/90214176/is-silicon-valleys-giant-foundation-just
-hoarding-money.

108 **in 2012 the *Fiscal Times*:** Blaire Briody, "10 Insanely Overpaid Nonprofit
Execs," *Fiscal Times*, December 20, 2012, https://www.thefiscaltimes.com
/Articles/2012/12/20/10-Insanely-Overpaid-Nonprofit-Execs.

108 **"Every nonprofit has two main jobs":** Sue Gardner, "What's *Really*
Wrong with Nonprofits—and How We Can Fix It," *Sue Gardner's Blog*,
October 20, 2013, https://suegardner.org/2013/10/20/whats-really-wrong
-with-nonprofits-and-how-we-can-fix-it/.

110 **"Indeed," wrote Jeffrey M. Berry:** Jeffery M. Berry and David F. Arons,

A Voice for Nonprofits (Washington DC: Brookings Institution Press, 2005).

111 **"With their funding restrictions"**: INCITE!, ed., *The Revolution Will Not Be Funded: Beyond the Non-Profit Industrial Complex* (Durham, NC: Duke University Press, 2017), xvi.

114 **"At a time when we need"**: Paul Klein, "Are Nonprofits Getting in the Way of Social Change?," *Stanford Social Innovation Review*, May 15, 2015, https://ssir.org/articles/entry/are_nonprofits_getting_in_the_way_of_ social_change.

5: #MEMETOO

120 **In October 2022, the *New York Times***: Brooks Barnes, "After #MeToo Reckoning, a Fear Hollywood Is Regressing," *New York Times*, October 24, 2022, https://www.nytimes.com/2022/10/24/business/media/holly wood-metoo.html.

120 **Depp, in turn, lost work:** Zac Ntim, "'Fantastic Beasts' Is Just the Start. Johnny Depp's Career Is Over, Experts Say," *Insider*, November 12, 2020, https://www.insider.com/fantastic-beasts-johnny-depp-career-is-over.

121 **As a *Vox* article stated:** Constance Grady, "The Me Too Backlash Is Here," *Vox*, June 2, 2022, https://www.vox.com/culture/23150632/johnny-depp -amber-heard-trial-verdict-me-too-backlash.

122 **Within two weeks of:** Amy Mackelden, "The TIME'S UP Legal Defense Fund Has Reached Its $15 Million Fundraising Goal," *Elle*, January 7, 2018, https://www.elle.com/culture/celebrities/a14769712/times-up-legal -defense-fund-reached-their-15-million-goal/.

122 **An October 2022 report:** Rebecca Keegan, "#MeToo, Five Years Later: Why Time's Up Imploded." *Hollywood Reporter*, October 3, 2022, https:// www.hollywoodreporter.com/news/general-news/metoo-five-years-later -times-up-1235228096/.

124 **The subhead of a *Washington Post***: Ashley Fetters Maloy and Paul Farhi, "Five Years On, What Happened to the Men of #MeToo?," *Washington Post*, October 16, 2022, https://www.washingtonpost.com/lifestyle/2022/10/16 /metoo-men-what-happened/.

125 **"Some of the most galvanizing":** Fetters Maloy and Farhi, "Five Years On."

127 **In 2018, in a small (and now defunct):** Katie Way, "I Went on a Date with Aziz Ansari. It Turned into the Worst Night of My Life." *Babe*, January 13, 2018, https://babe.net/2018/01/13/aziz-ansari-28355.

128 **For example, the feminist writer:** Jill Filipovic, "The Poorly Reported

Aziz Ansari Exposé Was a Missed Opportunity," *Guardian*, January 16, 2018, https://www.theguardian.com/commentisfree/2018/jan/16/aziz-ansari-story-missed-opportunity.

132   **Organizations like Time's Up were:** "Our Work," Time's Up, https://timesupnow.org/work/.

6: MEET THE GOODIES: WHY ARE LIBERALS THE WAY THEY ARE?

136   **A 2022 Gallup poll:** Lydia Saad, "U.S. Political Ideology Steady; Conservatives, Moderates Tie," Gallup, January 17, 2022, https://news.gallup.com/poll/388988/political-ideology-steady-conservatives-moderates-tie.aspx.

136   **A 2020 Pew poll:** Hannah Gilberstadt and Andrew Daniller, "Liberals Make Up the Largest Share of Democratic Voters, but Their Growth Has Slowed in Recent Years," Pew Research Center, January 17, 2020, https://www.pewresearch.org/fact-tank/2020/01/17/liberals-make-up-largest-share-of-democratic-voters/.

138   **"They turn nature into an achievement":** David Brooks, *Bobos in Paradise: The New Upper Class and How They Got There* (New York: Simon & Schuster, 2000), 212.

139   **"Locus of control, according to":** Richard B. Joelson, "Locus of Control," *Psychology Today*, August 2, 2017, https://www.psychologytoday.com/us/blog/moments-matter/201708/locus-control.

140   **"There is a strain of discourse":** Clare Coffey, "Failure to Cope 'Under Capitalism,'" *Gawker*, August 12, 2022, https://www.gawker.com/culture/failure-to-cope-under-capitalism.

142   **"It is still true that they":** David Brooks, *The Paradise Suite:* Bobos in Paradise *and* On Paradise Drive (New York: Simon & Schuster, 2011), ii.

143   **"American conservatives are more likely":** John Hood, "Psychology Helps Explain Political Divide," *Carolina Journal*, December 23, 2019, https://www.carolinajournal.com/opinion/psychology-helps-explain-political-divide/.

143   **a 1976 study found that:** Hanna Levenson and Jim Miller, "Multidimensional Locus of Control in Sociopolitical Activists of Conservative and Liberal Ideologies," *Journal of Personality and Social Psychology* 33, no. 2 (February 1976): 199–208.

144   **An analysis by the National:** Tom Wood, "The College Backgrounds of America's Talking Heads," National Association of Scholars, October 28, 2008, https://www.nas.org/blogs/article/the_college_backgrounds_of_americas_talking_heads.

144 **For example, a 2018 paper:** Jonathan Wai and Kaja Perina, "Expertise in Journalism: Factors Shaping a Cognitive and Culturally Elite Profession," *Journal of Expertise* 1, no. 1 (June 2018): 57–78.

144 **Some of the most important work:** Thomas Piketty, *Capital in the Twenty-First Century* (Cambridge, MA: Harvard University Press, 2014).

145 **Piketty's 2018 article "Brahmin":** Thomas Piketty, "Brahmin Left vs Merchant Right: Rising Inequality and the Changing Structure of Political Conflict," WID.world Working Paper 7, 2018.

145 **the paper found that income:** "Educated Voters' Leftward Shift Is Surprisingly Old and International," *The Economist*, May 29, 2021, https://www.economist.com/graphic-detail/2021/05/29/educated-voters-leftward-shift-is-surprisingly-old-and-international.

145 **In September 2021, Nate Cohn:** Nate Cohn, "How Educational Differences Are Widening America's Political Rift," *New York Times,* September 8, 2021, https://www.nytimes.com/2021/09/08/us/politics/how-college-graduates-vote.html.

146 **Writing for the Mellon Foundation:** Paula McAvoy, David Campbell, and Diana Hess, "The Relationship Between a Liberal Arts Education and Democratic Outcomes," Mellon Foundation, January 2019, https://mellon.org/news-blog/articles/relationship-between-liberal-arts-education-and-democratic-outcomes/.

146 **turnout for high school graduates:** "Voting and Registration in the Election of 2020," United States Census Bureau, April 2021, https://www.census.gov/data/tables/time-series/demo/voting-and-registration/p20-585.html.

146 **And they're more likely:** See, among many other studies: Jacob R. Brown, Ryan D. Enos, James Felgenbaum, and Soumyajit Mazumder, "Childhood Cross-Ethnic Exposure Predicts Political Behavior Seven Decades Later: Evidence from Linked Administrative Data." *Science Advances* 7, no. 24 (June 2021), https://www.science.org/doi/10.1126/sciadv.abe8432.

147 **But recent high-quality research:** Ralph Scott, "Does University Make You More Liberal? Estimating the Within-Individual Effects of Higher Education on Political Values," *Electoral Studies* 77 (June 2022), 102471.

147 **Reviewing the literature for *New York*:** Eric Levitz, "How the Diploma Divide Is Remaking American Politics," *New York*, October 19, 2022, https://nymag.com/intelligencer/2022/10/education-polarization-diploma-divide-democratic-party-working-class.html.

149 **According to the Bureau of Labor Statistics:** U.S. Bureau of Labor Statistics, "News Analysts, Reporters, and Journalists," *Occupational Outlook*

Handbook, U.S. Department of Labor, accessed September 8, 2022, https://
www.bls.gov/ooh/media-and-communication/reporters-correspondents
-and-broadcast-news-analysts.htm.

149 **In academia, according to:** Dr. Kelly S. Meier, "Salary of a Tenure Track
Professor," *Chron*, March 12, 2019, https://work.chron.com/salary-tenure
-track-professor-7796.html.

151 **In our university system:** Leslie Davis and Richard Fry, "College Faculty
Have Become More Racially and Ethnically Diverse, but Remain Far Less
So than Students," Pew Research Center, July 31, 2019, https://www.pew
research.org/fact-tank/2019/07/31/us-college-faculty-student-diversity/.

151 **According to the News Leaders Association's:** "2019 Diversity Survey,"
News Leaders Association, September 10, 2019, https://www.newsleaders
.org/2019-diversity-survey-results.

151 **Meanwhile, only 11 percent of top editors:** Rasmus Kleis Nielsen, Meera
Selva, and Simge Andi, "Race and Leadership in the News Media 2020:
Evidence from Five Markets," Reuters, July 16, 2020, https://reutersinstitute
.politics.ox.ac.uk/race-and-leadership-news-media-2020-evidence-five
-markets.

155 **In 2016, I described:** Fredrik deBoer, "Elena Ferrante and the Politics of
Deference," *Towner*, October 26, 2016.

155 **In his 2022 book,** *Elite Capture*: Táíwò, *Elite Capture*, 69.

160 **"Since the '60s":** Ed Gordon and Shelby Steele, "'White Guilt' and the
End of the Civil Rights Era," transcript, *NPR*, May 5, 2006, https://www
.npr.org/templates/story/story.php?storyId=5385701.

7: WHY IS CLASS FIRST?

165 **Referencing the tweet,** *The Atlantic*'s: Clare Foran, "Hillary Clinton's
Intersectional Politics," *The Atlantic*, March 9, 2016, https://www.theatlantic
.com/politics/archive/2016/03/hillary-clinton-intersectionality/472872/.

166 **In March 2016, the Clinton:** Hari Ziyad, "Democratic Candidates Had
a Chance to Prove Bona Fides on Race. They Failed," *Guardian*, January
12, 2016, https://www.theguardian.com/commentisfree/2016/jan/12/demo
cratic-presidential-candidates-black-and-brown-forum-iowa-primary.

166 **In January 2016,** *The Guardian*'s: Ziyad, "Democratic Candidates Had a
Chance."

167 **As *Reason* magazine pointed out:** Robby Soave, "Former Clinton Campaign Staffer Accuses Bernie Sanders of Failing to Mention Race, Gender
in Speech That Explicitly Mentioned Race, Gender," *Reason*, March 4,

2019, https://reason.com/2019/03/04/bernie-sanders-zerlina-maxwell -race-gend/.

167 **But it is the case that:** See, for one: Blair L. M. Kelley, "Biden Has Black Voters' Support Over Sanders, and It's Not Because They're Moderates," *NBC News*, March 5, 2020, https://www.nbcnews.com/think/opinion /biden-has-black-voters-support-over-sanders-it-s-not-ncna1150576.

167 **"In every one of the 27 primaries":** John Hudak, "Why Bernie Sanders Vastly Underperformed in the 2020 Primary," Brookings, March 20, 2020, https://www.brookings.edu/blog/fixgov/2020/03/20/why-bernie-sanders -vastly-underperformed-in-the-2020-primary/.

169 **"The label 'class reductionist'":** Asad Haider, "How Calling Someone a 'Class Reductionist' Became a Lefty Insult," *Salon*, July 25, 2020, https:// www.salon.com/2020/07/25/how-calling-someone-a-class-reductionist -became-a-lefty-insult/.

169 **"class reductionism is the supposed view":** Adolph Reed Jr., "The Myth of Class Reductionism," *New Republic*, September 25, 2019, https://new republic.com/article/154996/myth-class-reductionism.

170 **In *Elite Capture*:** Táíwò, *Elite Capture*, 111.

171 **"Politics today, however, is defined":** Francis Fukuyama, "Against Identity Politics: The New Tribalism and the Crisis of Democracy," *Foreign Affairs* 97, no. 5 (September 2018): 90–114.

175 **"According to Marx":** Renzo Llorente, "Marx's Concept of 'Universal Class': A Rehabilitation," *Science & Society* 77, no. 4 (October 2013): 536–60.

175 **As the socialist historian Eric Hobsbawm:** Eric Hobsbawm, "Identity Politics and the Left," *New Left Review* (May/June 1996): 38–47.

181 **"the premise of this style of argument":** Marc Novicoff, "Stop Marketing Race-Blind Policies as Racial Equity Initiatives," *Slow Boring*, February 20, 2021, https://www.slowboring.com/p/race-blind-policies-racial-equity.

182 **"Slums with hundreds of thousands":** King, "MLK's Forgotten Call."

185 **"Hispanic Voters Are Normie Voters":** Ruy Teixeira, "Hispanic Voters Are Normie Voters," *Liberal Patriot*, August 11, 2022, https://www.liberal patriot.com/p/hispanic-voters-are-normie-voters.

187 **Writing in *Jacobin*—frequently:** Paul Heideman, "Class Rules Every- thing Around Me," *Jacobin*, May 3, 2019, https://jacobin.com/2019/05 /working-class-structure-oppression-capitalist-identity.

192 **As the American sociologist:** Todd Gitlin, *The Twilight of Common Dreams: Why America Is Wracked By Culture Wars* (New York: Metro- politan Books, 1995), 165.

8: TO FIGHT FOR EVERYONE

194 **But for most of us:** Bureau of Labor Statistics, "Union Members—2022," US Department of Labor, January 19, 2023, https://www.bls.gov/news .release/pdf/union2.pdf.

199 **Yet, to pick one example:** Gabriel Arana, "White Gay Men Are Hindering Our Progress as a Queer Community," *them*, November 9, 2017, https:// www.them.us/story/white-gay-men-are-hindering-our-progress.

INDEX

ABOUT THE AUTHOR

FREDRIK ᴅᴇ**BOER** is a writer and academic.